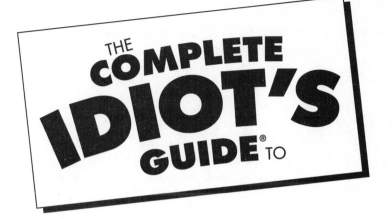

THE
COMPLETE
IDIOT'S
GUIDE® TO

Snack Cakes

by Leslie Bilderback, CMB,
with photographs by James O. Fraioli

ALPHA

A member of Penguin Group (USA) Inc.

This book is dedicated to my favorite snackers, Bill, Emma, and Claire. Eat an apple from time to time, will ya!

ALPHA BOOKS

Published by the Penguin Group

Penguin Group (USA) Inc., 375 Hudson Street, New York, New York 10014, USA

Penguin Group (Canada), 90 Eglinton Avenue East, Suite 700, Toronto, Ontario M4P 2Y3, Canada (a division of Pearson Penguin Canada Inc.)

Penguin Books Ltd., 80 Strand, London WC2R 0RL, England

Penguin Ireland, 25 St. Stephen's Green, Dublin 2, Ireland (a division of Penguin Books Ltd.)

Penguin Group (Australia), 250 Camberwell Road, Camberwell, Victoria 3124, Australia (a division of Pearson Australia Group Pty. Ltd.)

Penguin Books India Pvt. Ltd., 11 Community Centre, Panchsheel Park, New Delhi—110 017, India

Penguin Group (NZ), 67 Apollo Drive, Rosedale, North Shore, Auckland 1311, New Zealand (a division of Pearson New Zealand Ltd.)

Penguin Books (South Africa) (Pty.) Ltd., 24 Sturdee Avenue, Rosebank, Johannesburg 2196, South Africa

Penguin Books Ltd., Registered Offices: 80 Strand, London WC2R 0RL, England

International Standard Book Number: 978-1-59257-737-8
Library of Congress Catalog Card Number: 2007941343

10   09   08   8   7   6   5   4   3   2   1

Interpretation of the printing code: The rightmost number of the first series of numbers is the year of the book's printing; the rightmost number of the second series of numbers is the number of the book's printing. For example, a printing code of 08-1 shows that the first printing occurred in 2008.

Printed in the United States of America

Note: This publication contains the opinions and ideas of its author. It is intended to provide helpful and informative material on the subject matter covered. It is sold with the understanding that the author and publisher are not engaged in rendering professional services in the book. If the reader requires personal assistance or advice, a competent professional should be consulted.

The author and publisher specifically disclaim any responsibility for any liability, loss, or risk, personal or otherwise, which is incurred as a consequence, directly or indirectly, of the use and application of any of the contents of this book.

Most Alpha books are available at special quantity discounts for bulk purchases for sales promotions, premiums, fund-raising, or educational use. Special books, or book excerpts, can also be created to fit specific needs.

For details, write: Special Markets, Alpha Books, 375 Hudson Street, New York, NY 10014.

Publisher: *Marie Butler-Knight*
Editorial Director: *Mike Sanders*
Senior Managing Editor: *Billy Fields*
Senior Acquisitions Editor: *Paul Dinas*
Development Editor: *Ginny Munroe*
Senior Production Editor: *Janette Lynn*

Copy Editor: *Lisanne V. Jensen*
Cover Designer: *Kurt Owens*
Book Designer: *Trina Wurst*
Indexer: *Brad Herriman*
Layout: *Ayanna Lacey*
Proofreader: *John Etchison*

Contents at a Glance

Contents

Introduction

You're hungry. You have a sweet tooth. You have company coming. You need to contribute to a bake sale. You want to impress that cutie down the hall. But you have little time, little patience, and even less skill. Where will you turn?

Snack cakes to the rescue!

These desserts are the staples of bake sales, church socials, picnic lunches, and after-school snacks. Within this category are hundreds of recipes in every flavor imaginable. The one thing they all have in common is simplicity. You don't need fancy equipment or decorating skills. You don't need a culinary degree or a subscription to *Gourmet* magazine. All you need is some basic ingredients and about an hour.

These cakes are designed to please everyone—especially the baker. Even if you have never baked in your life, you'll be able to pull off a snack cake. And once you start, you'll be hooked—because everybody loves cake—and by association, everyone will love you, too!

Snack History

When most people hear the phrase "snack cake," they immediately think of one thing: the Twinkie. This twentieth-century icon of junk food has been the king of snack cakes since its creation in the 1930s. An inventive baker created the product to utilize strawberry shortcake equipment that lay dormant when strawberries were out of season. The Twinkie was originally filled with banana cream but was replaced with vanilla when bananas were rationed during World War II. Reintroduced in recent years, Banana Twinkies are enjoying a resurgence of popularity. Legend has it that the name was inspired by an ad for Twinkle-Toe Shoes.

While it is certainly the most recognizable, the Twinkie does not stand alone in the land of snack cakes. The Moon Pie was created even earlier to fulfill the lunch-box needs of construction workers at the turn of the twentieth century.

The first Little Debbie cake, an oatmeal cookie sandwiched with cream filling called an Oatmeal Pie, hit the scene in the 1960s. The name and logo image was inspired by the founder's four-year-old granddaughter, her play clothes, and her favorite straw hat.

In 1937, the founder of the Interstate Bakery Corporation introduced cakes good enough to serve in the White House and dubbed them Dolly Madison. The first lady, wife of President James Madison, was well known as a domestic goddess. Her name has a long association with everything for the home, including linens, dinnerware, jewelry, tobacco, and a variety of foods. She was the original hostess with the mostest and served as our nation's social matron. You could call her the original Martha Stewart. Original advertising for the Dolly Madison Bakery brand included images of a prim and proper nineteenth-century woman caring for her home.

When women started to work outside the home, Dolly Madison Bakery decided to change their target. Individual cakes, including Zingers, Gems, and Fruit Pies, were marketed to kids with the help of Charles Schultz's *Peanuts* comic strip. Dolly Madison became a major sponsor of the *Peanuts* television specials and quickly became a household name. Each product had a different character on its wrapper, and their individual wrapping made them perfect for lunch boxes. Charlie Brown preached the back-to-school message, "School time is snack time."

Here, with *Peanuts* and lunch boxes, lies the key to our love of the snack cake. They are permanently linked in our sensory memory with the joys of childhood. For so many of us, these cakes are not merely junk food. They are heartwarming comfort food.

A Better Hostess

Sadly, today we also recognize the lack of nutritional benefits of these products. Their shelf lives are the stuff of urban legend, and knowing what goes in them to prolong their shelf lives is enough to make you lose your appetite.

Individual cellophane wrappers lulled our nation into a false sense of security. Small, personal servings allude to portion control. Sure, they're indulgent. But they're small. Besides, we all know that just one won't hurt.

The result? Snack cakes are no-no's. They are the epitome of empty calories. These delightful creations, once the liberator of busy moms, are now relegated to convenience stores and gas stations in easy reach of late-night munchers—providing the finishing touch to a repast of nachos and slushies. Any self-respecting mother knows to hide the snack cakes at the bottom of the shopping cart lest she run into the vegetarian-yoga instructor-PTA president at the market.

Nutritional knowledge and a health-conscious society have sent the snack cake into hiding.

The solution: homemade.

There is no need to give up snack cakes entirely. They can absolutely become a part of your family's comfort food repertoire—and your own culinary legacy—when you bake them yourself.

Real butter, eggs, sugar, and flour produce an unmistakable result. No rubbery texture, no greasy filling, no mysterious aftertaste here. Just pure, unadulterated scratch baking. Not even box mixes can replicate the distinctive quality of homemade. Best of all, with homemade, you know what you're eating.

And nothing lights up a room like homemade cake. Recognizable for their imperfections, they will always receive ooh's and ahh's and be the first to vanish from the buffet. Everyone prefers a homemade cake to the über-sweet, drearily uniform, Crisco-frosted, grocery store variety. That's because the homemade cake has become unusual. Part of its value is its scarcity.

Baking from Scratch

The joy of scratch baking is sadly unfamiliar to modern generations. Our ready-made, frozen-concentrated, drive-thru, instant, freeze-dried culture has made scratch baking scarce and somewhat extraordinary. Today, the effort of baking from scratch is almost more impressive than the cake itself.

Sure, you're busy. Your family is on the go, and you cannot afford the time to bake. I have but one response. You can't afford *not* to bake!

Baking provides more than simply frivolous treats. It can be a relaxing respite from your everyday existence. For many, it is a creative outlet. Cook as a family and bring everyone together, working toward the common goal of gleeful cupcakes, indulgent brownies, and amusing doughnuts. Baking is an exercise in chemistry, math, and self-control. It can only make you a better person.

Within these pages, you will find a plethora of snack cake ideas and all the skills needed to complete them successfully. Part 1 will prepare you to shop with a complete understanding of ingredients and equipment. Then, you'll learn the proper methods of mixing, baking, and frosting. Part 2 consists of cupcakes, both fun and frivolous. Part 3 examines the world of bars, brownies, and squares—with sticky and sophisticated recipes from the past and present. Part 4 contains sweet dough recipes, including classic yeast bread, cream puffs, and doughnuts. Part 5 includes all the mini cakes and tarts you loved as a kid—along with some grown-up options.

Throughout these pages, you'll find sidebars to help make the most of your time in the kitchen. *Sweet Talk* sidebars provide explanations of cooking terminology. *Helpful Hints* sidebars provide shortcuts and ideas to make the recipes easier. *Heads Up* sidebars warn you of potential goof-ups, and *Tidbits* sidebars are full of interesting facts pertaining to the recipe at hand. At the end of the book, you'll find a glossary and a list of resources for purchasing fun equipment and ingredients.

Unwrapping a store-bought snack cake will never allow you to bask in the glory of your creation. So dust off your apron and prepare to be the belle of the baking ball. It's never too late to start a family baking tradition. You could conceivably find a specialty, become known for your baking prowess, and even create your own secret recipe.

Go ahead. Indulge in a little snack cakery.

Extras

Sweet Talk

Here you'll find definitions and explanations of specific culinary phrases

Heads Up

These cautionary sidebars will alert you to common mistakes and possible goof-ups.

Tidbits

Here you'll find all the fascinating history, important culinary references, and useless trivia that makes cooking fun.

Helpful Hints

These sidebars are loaded with timesaving tips and tricks to take the "ACK" out of snack cakes.

Acknowledgments

Baking is only fun when you have someone to bake for. If it weren't for my cake-loving family, I would never even bother. You guys make my life sweet as can be.

Trademarks

All terms mentioned in this book that are known to be or are suspected of being trademarks or service marks have been appropriately capitalized. Alpha Books and Penguin Group (USA) Inc. cannot attest to the accuracy of this information. Use of a term in this book should not be regarded as affecting the validity of any trademark or service mark.

Part 1

Basic Techniques

Baking is not difficult, and snack cakes in particular are at the easy end of the pastry spectrum. But regardless of the level of difficulty, there are a few basic techniques that will ensure your products turn out as perfect as possible.

Buying the right ingredients is the first step toward creating successful snack cakes. There are lots of options, but only a few will yield the best results. Then, once you have the right ingredients, it's important to put them together in the right way. Proper mixing, pans, and oven temperatures all contribute to a successful result. Finally, this section includes all the best frosting, filling, and topping recipes—the crowning glory of your snack masterpieces.

Basic Ingredients and Mixing

In This Chapter

- ◆ Choosing the right ingredients
- ◆ Understanding the role of ingredients in baked goods
- ◆ Using proper techniques for the best possible outcome

Not many ingredients are needed to create delicious cakes, but in order to make the cakes superb, the ingredients should be of high quality. For every ingredient, there are often several options available at any supermarket. The recipes in this book call for ingredients that should be your first choice. Using these ingredients will produce the finest outcome. Other foods may be substituted, but the result will be less delicious.

Flour

For the most part, people stock all-purpose flour in their pantries. It lives up to its name and can be used for any recipe in this book. Certain recipes, however, specify cake flour or bread flour depending on whether a lighter or a more durable dough or batter is required. Both of these flours are available at most supermarkets.

Cake Flour

For delicate cakes and pastries, cake flour is the flour of choice. It contains more starch and less protein than all-purpose flour, and the resulting baked goods turn out lighter and more tender than they do when made with all-purpose flour. As the name indicates, this flour is used primarily for cakes but also is found in some pastry dough recipes. Pastry flour is a similar alternative, with a similar protein/starch ratio, but is a little harder to find. Cake flour is readily available in supermarkets— usually in a bright red box.

Bread Flour

At the other end of the flour spectrum, bread flour contains less starch and more protein than all-purpose flour. The protein in flour is called *gluten*, a substance that—when moistened and kneaded—becomes elastic. This elasticity is essential when making yeast breads. It enables the dough to rise by trapping the gas of fermentation: carbon dioxide. This gas creates bubbles in the dough that become the crumb in bread that we know and love. When shopping for bread flour, look for "Bread Flour," "Better for Bread," or "High Gluten" on the label.

Sweet Talk

Gluten is a mixture of two proteins found in the endosperm of grains, including wheat, rye, and barley. About 1 percent of Americans are sensitive to gluten, and must adhere to a strict gluten-free diet. Luckily, there are many gluten-free products available, and more coming every day.

Whole-Wheat Flour

Similar in its makeup to all-purpose flour, whole-wheat flour has the added bonus of containing both wheat bran and germ—making it a more nutritious choice. It can generally be substituted in any recipe that calls for all-purpose flour, but be advised that the taste and texture will be altered.

Whole-wheat flour is made by blending wheat germ and bran, first removed during the milling of all-purpose flour, with white flour. If you want flour milled from the whole grain, look for "Stone Ground" on the label.

Sugar

When a recipe calls for sugar, it means granulated white sugar. If another sugar is called for, it will be specified.

Granulated Sugar

Commonly referred to as white sugar, granulated sugar is made both from sugar cane and sugar beets. They are generally interchangeable, although cane sugar is preferable for candy work as it tends to crystallize less than beet sugar.

Brown Sugar

Simply white sugar that has molasses added to it, brown sugar was traditionally less-refined sugar. Today, the manufacturing process makes it more economically feasible to refine it all, then add molasses (which was removed during refining) back in. Light brown sugar has less molasses (and less flavor) than dark brown sugar. They are interchangeable, and their use should be determined by your taste preferences.

Brown sugar should always be packed firmly into measuring cups. Brown and white sugar can be used interchangeably. The flavor will be altered but not the texture or chemistry of the batter or dough.

Molasses

This byproduct of the sugar refinement process is widely used for its flavor and color. Unsulphured molasses is considered the finest quality and is made from the first boiling of well-ripened sugar cane. Sulphured molasses is made from green sugar cane that is treated with sulphur dioxide during extraction, which acts as a preservative. Blackstrap molasses is made during the subsequent boiling—and while it has less sugar, it contains large amounts of micronutrients, including vitamin B6, iron, calcium, magnesium, and potassium. It is commonly used as a diet supplement as well as in cattle feed and large-scale food manufacturing. Molasses from sugar beets is a different product, low in sugar, high in salts, and unpalatable to humans. It is highly nutritious, and is therefore reserved for livestock.

Powdered Sugar

Also known as confectioner's sugar and icing sugar, powdered sugar is granulated white sugar ground down to a powder with added corn-starch to inhibit clumping. There are different granulations available in specialty stores, and they are labeled with numbers that designate the grain size. Higher numbers indicate a finer grain. Basic powdered sugar at the supermarket is generally 10X and is adequate for all recipes. Powdered sugar may be used in place of white sugar to sweeten recipes but granulated white sugar will not provide the same texture in baked goods that powdered sugar does.

Honey

Made by bees, honey is a naturally occurring sweetener that needs no refinement. It can be substituted for granulated sugar as a sweetener, but it is twice as sweet—so use half as much.

Artificial Sweeteners

There are a number of sugar substitutes on the market, and most can be used in place of sugar with good results. Consult the packaging for exact substitution ratios as each product differs.

Salt

Salt brings out the natural flavors of foods. Its chemistry enters the taste buds quickly, opening them up for the other elements in the food. Salt is used in pretty much all recipes—not to make the food taste salty but to enhance the natural flavors of the other ingredients.

All recipes in this book call for kosher salt, which is readily available in supermarkets. Kosher salt contains no iodine, chemicals, or starches and consequently has a more pure, less metallic flavor than regular table salt. It generally has a coarser texture, with flat crystals that dissolve quickly. A finer grind of kosher salt is now available for use in salt shakers. Common table salt is generally iodized. Potassium iodide is added as a dietary supplement to prevent iodine deficiency, a major cause of goiter and cretinism. Most table salt has a water-absorbing additive to keep it from clumping, and some countries add fluoride as well. Table salt may be used instead of kosher salt, but if you have never used kosher salt, consider giving it a try. It is used universally by chefs for its superior flavor.

Fancy salt—like sea salt, marsh salt, and fleur de sel—can be used but are not necessary. The expense of these salts is wasted in recipes that have a multitude of ingredients. Reserve them for dishes that feature the salt, perhaps sprinkled over fresh vegetables or meats.

Leaveners

Leaveners are the ingredients that allow cakes and betters to rise. In the old days, yeast and air were the only leaveners available to the home baker. Air could only be incorporated through lots of elbow grease, and yeast had to be harvested at home, using a starter. Today, we have chemical leaveners, machinery to help us incorporate air, and store-bought yeast, ready to use.

Yeast

Yeast is a living organism that occurs naturally in the air all around us. It was first utilized around 3000 B.C. for the fermentation of beer and wine, and soon after it was harvested to leaven pastes of grain mash. Knowledge of yeast led to the development of yeast starters, which was the only way to make bread until the twentieth century. It wasn't until the invention of the microscope in the mid-1800s when humans figured out yeast was responsible for fermentation. Once it was isolated, commercial production of yeast began and revolutionized baking.

Yeast works by feeding on carbohydrates in a warm, moist environment. When these conditions are optimal, the yeast produces a byproduct: carbon dioxide. This process is called fermentation. The carbon dioxide is trapped within the dough thanks to the gluten, causing the dough to expand.

The key to this process is carbohydrates—found in flour and often added in simple sugar form (granulated sugar or honey) at the start of a bread recipe—to jump-start the process. The moisture is crucial in the conversion of complex carbohydrates of flour to simple carbs. Warmth speeds up the entire process, but it is not essential. The fermentation will take place without it, but it will take longer. Longer fermentation is often preferred by bread bakers because it produces more flavor than a quick rise. This is the theory behind sourdough bread.

Chemical Leaveners

For cakes without yeast, early bakers had only air as a leavener (beaten in by hand). Old recipes call for batters to be beaten for 300 to 400 strokes or more to create such delicacies as pound cake. Today, we have chemicals to help.

Baking soda is *bicarbonate of soda*. When added to acid, it releases carbon dioxide gas. (Remember the papier-mâché volcano trick from elementary school science?) When mixed into batters with acidic ingredients like vinegar, sour cream, or buttermilk, the gas accumulates and leavens the product.

Baking powder, first marketed in the 1860s, is bicarbonate of soda with an acidic ingredient already mixed in (usually cream of tartar or calcium phosphate). When baking powder is mixed into a recipe, it reacts with the moisture of the batter and the heat of the oven to produce carbon dioxide. The gas builds up and raises the product. Double-acting baking powder begins this process when moistened but holds a portion of the reaction until heat is applied. The original baking powder,

> **Sweet Talk**
>
> **Bicarbonate of soda** is a chemical compound created when ammonia is used to separate the sodium (Na) from the chloride (Cl) of salt (NaCl) in the presence of carbon dioxide and water.

single-acting, releases all the carbon dioxide with moisture and must therefore be baked immediately upon mixing.

Air

Air also is used as a leavener—added to batters by heavy beating or in the form of an egg foam. By whipping eggs (whole, yolks, or whites) and carefully folding them into the batter without deflating, the air is trapped and expands in the heat of the oven. This leavener is used in foam cakes such as sponge and angel food, as well as soufflés.

Fats

Fats are added to recipes to tenderize, moisten, and prolong shelf life. Because their consistency is altered by heating, fats should be used with care at the temperature indicated in the recipe.

In most cases, recipes in this book call for unsalted butter. Available in supermarkets, unsalted butter is preferred by most bakers and chefs for its superior flavor. The lack of salt gives the cook control over the amount of salt in a recipe. Salted butter can always be detected because it makes the dish saltier than necessary. If you have no choice but to use salted butter, don't forget to omit the salt from the recipe.

Margarine is never called for in this book because it produces inferior products and is an unhealthy food. It is made from artificially saturated vegetable oil via a process called hydrogenation. Hydrogenation produces trans-fatty acids, which have been shown to be a major cause of coronary artery disease, obesity, and some forms of cancer.

Margarine also creates an unpleasant aftertaste. Animal fats melt at body temperatures, but vegetable fats do not. Vegetable fat coats the tongue and lingers on the palate long after the food is swallowed.

Butter, although a saturated animal-based fat, is preferable to margarine in maintaining a healthy diet. However, problems occur with any saturated fats when eaten in excess. They are the healthier alternative but should still be eaten in moderation (as all fats should be).

Oils used in these recipes generally have a neutral flavor, which means their flavor will not overpower a recipe. For healthful baking, look for the good *polyunsaturated fats*. Olive oil, while a healthy choice, has too strong a flavor. It would give an odd taste to a dessert like chocolate cake. The recipes in this book generally call for peanut or canola oil. Other oils, like safflower, corn, or vegetable, can be substituted—but keep in mind the flavor of the dish being prepared.

Lard is a common ingredient in pie dough. It is easily cut into dry ingredients and creates a superior flakiness that cannot be achieved with butter or shortening. It is generally rendered from pork and thus is not a kosher food.

Eggs

When a recipe calls for eggs (in this book and every other book), it is calling for large eggs. Very rarely will a recipe specify a medium, extra-large, or jumbo egg. If you find you must make a substitution, weigh the eggs. A large, whole egg weighs about 2 ounces: the white weighs 1 ounce, and the yolk weighs just over $2/3$ ounces. Egg substitutes should be used in the same manner, weighing them according to the weight of the egg in the recipe.

Generally, two whites are equivalent to two yolks and in most cases are interchangeable. Excess whites will yield a rubbery, dryer product while excess yolks will make the product richer, fattier, and darker yellow.

Dairy

Milk and milk products are common ingredients in baked goods. They lend fat, protein, sugar (lactose), and moisture to batters and doughs—all crucial components of any snack cake.

When a recipe calls for milk, it can be any milk you prefer to use. Whole milk is the fattiest choice and will produce a slightly richer product than using nonfat milk. But nonfat has all the essential components and can be used interchangeably.

Cream is available in most markets as *whipping* or *heavy*. The difference is in the fat content, which varies by producer. Whipping cream is usually *light whipping cream*, which contains about 30 percent fat. *Light cream* is sometimes available, with as low as 18 percent fat. Heavy whipping cream, which works best for whipping, usually contains about 35 percent fat. Professionals use *manufacturing cream*, which has the highest fat content of all (more than 40 percent). All of these creams are interchangeable in recipes. The benefit of higher-fat creams is their richer flavor and the ease in which they whip up.

Buttermilk used to be the byproduct of churning butter, but today it is simply milk with an added culture to make it sour. Small bits of butter are added to give it an authentic look. Buttermilk and sour cream appear as an acidic ingredient in many recipes that contain baking soda. They can be used interchangeably, although the texture of the batter will be thicker when sour cream is used. Plain yogurt also can be used in this instance, as can milk with added lemon juice or vinegar.

> **Heads Up**
>
> If a recipe calls for buttermilk, it probably also contains baking soda, and needs the acid to create leavening reaction. Regular milk will not do as a substitute, as it contains no acid.

Flavorings

Many foods are added to batter and dough solely for flavor. They can generally be used interchangeably and cause no major problems when added in larger or smaller quantities.

Vanilla

Vanilla is by far the most common pastry flavoring. Used mainly in extract form, it is made from beans harvested from a tropical orchid. Most extract is made from Madagascar vanilla, but you also can find vanilla extract made from Tahitian and Mexican beans.

Tidbits

Bourbon vanilla is not made from bourbon, but is Madagascar vanilla. When Spanish explorers brought the beans back to Europe, the French tried to propagate the orchids on the Island of Bourbon, now called Réunion.

The beans contain thousands of tiny black seeds that carry the flavorful oil. To use a bean, slice it lengthwise, scrape out the seeds, and add them to the recipe in place of extract. The appearance of tiny black specks will indicate that real vanilla was used. One quarter to one half pod will flavor most recipes adequately, but you can add as much or as little as your taste prefers.

When buying extract, avoid imitation vanilla—which is less flavorful and usually requires using more to achieve the flavor effect of the real stuff. Extracts also are available in many flavors other than vanilla, but most have a distinctly artificial flavor. Be aware of the strength of your extracts. Use what is called for in a recipe first, and taste before deciding to add more.

Zest

Citrus zest is a common flavoring in many baked goods. Zest is the outermost rind of citrus fruit. This outer, colorful skin contains the essential oils and flavor compounds that flavor the fruit itself and add strong citrus flavor to foods.

The best way to remove zest is to grate it using the finest holes of a cheese grater or a microplane. A zester is a tool that removes long strings of zest, which must then be chopped finely before they are added to a recipe. A vegetable peeler can be used in a similar fashion. The finer the zest is chopped, the more flavor will be released into a recipe. Avoid the white pith underneath the zest but outside the fruit pulp; it's bitter.

Helpful Hints

Zest can be grated and stored for several months in the freezer for later use.

Nuts

Nuts can be folded into batters, used as a topping, or ground into butter and added as a fatty ingredient. They are loaded with oil, so care should be taken to keep them from turning rancid. Leftovers should be used quickly or stored in the refrigerator for extended periods.

Nuts always taste best when toasted. This task is best done in an oven. Spread them out on a baking sheet and roast at 350°F for 5 to 10 minutes until their aroma fills the kitchen. Cool toasted nuts completely before adding them to a recipe.

Spices and Herbs

Spices are the dried seeds, berries, or bark of plants. They are generally ground but can be bought whole and ground at home for more flavor and a longer shelf life. Herbs are the green leaves and stems of plants and can also be bought dry or grown and used fresh.

Incorporation

Besides the ingredients, combining them is the most important element of a recipe. If ingredients are combined in the wrong order, a recipe will definitely have an altered texture. There are several procedures that come up again and again in recipes, and understanding them is key to successful baking.

Creaming

This term is used to describe the beating together of fat and sugar until it is smooth. In this step, it is important to get all the lumps out of the fat—and the sugar crystals help to do that. If the lumps are not taken out here, they will never come out.

Sifting

This procedure is used not only to remove lumps from dry ingredients but also to lighten and add air, which in turn lightens the finished product. Sifting can be done in a traditional barrel sifter or through a wire mesh strainer. If no sifter is available, stir the ingredients around with a whisk to break them up and add a little air.

Adding Alternately

This term is used to describe the method of adding dry and wet ingredients into a batter. They are added separately so that incorporation is easy and even. Both dry and wet ingredients are divided into two or three batches. A little of the dry mixture is added and worked in completely. Then, a little bit of the wet mixture is added and worked in completely. This process repeats until all ingredients are added. This slow incorporation, with careful, thorough blending in between, is the best way to create an even, well-mixed batter.

Stirring, Mixing, and Beating

These steps require no special technique. The purpose is simply to combine ingredients. Beating usually implies some muscle is required, and some portion of air will be incorporated—although not as much as whipping implies. Beating may also refer to the removal of lumps, as in creaming.

Whipping

This method is meant to be done with a whisk, either by hand or with an electric handheld or stand mixer. Whisks incorporate air into a batter or ingredient as they move, and this air increases the volume of a mixture. Air trapped within a batter will also leaven a product that is baked. When air is heated, it expands—taking the batter with it.

Whipped foods are described by peak stage. To determine the stage, lift the whisk out of the bowl and hold the mixture so that its drips, or peaks, point up. If the peak bends way over, it is a soft peak. If it bends over a little, it is a medium peak. If the peak stands upright, it is a stiff peak. This rule works for egg whites as well as cream.

Folding

Folding is a gentle method of combining two ingredients. It is generally used when one of the components is a *foam*. Folding allows for thorough incorporation with as few strokes as possible. The more strokes the foam is subjected to, the more air is forced out. The foam then becomes deflated, and the mixture is no longer light. In the case of cakes or soufflés, this means they will not rise adequately.

When folding with a rubber spatula or spoon, each pass through the batter drags a little foam with it. For faster incorporation and less deflation, fold with a wire whisk. With 30 to 40 wires, each pass drags 30 or 40 times the amount of foam through.

For an efficient fold, think of the bowl as a clock and pass the whisk down through the batter from 12 o'clock to 6 o'clock. Then, turn the bowl counterclockwise and bring the whisk back out at 9 o'clock. Repeat three to four more times, folding through a new area of the batter with each pass. The batter should be fairly well blended but still have the thickness and body of the foam. If the batter becomes thin or watery, you have folded too much and should consider starting again.

Lightening

This term is used to describe thinning out a batter before a more delicate ingredient, usually a foam, is folded in. A small portion of the foam—usually no more than a third—is folded into the batter first, which thins it out. Then, the remaining foam is folded in all at once. This process allows the delicate foam to incorporate more easily with less deflation.

The Cut-In Technique

This is a method of incorporating fat and flour together—not by beating or creaming but by crumbling. The butter and flour do not actually combine but remain separate; the butter in small chunks floating within the flour. It should never look like a paste. This peaceful coexistence of fat and flour is the key to tender, flaky baked goods. In the oven, the moisture contained within the fat evaporates into steam, pushing up the dough and leaving little pockets of air that our mouths read as flakiness.

To get your butter small while still keeping it from melting and joining with the flour into a paste, keep the ingredients cold. Freeze the diced butter before adding it, and if the temperature is particularly warm, freeze the flour for 10 to 15 minutes.

> **Sweet Talk** _____
>
> The **pastry blender** is a tool used to break fat into flour. It's been used for decades, so if you don't have one, your grandma probably does. It consists of a bow made of multiple wires connected to a handle.

Using your fingers to break down the butter makes it easier to monitor the butter's size. Many bakers keep their hands out of the mix entirely, preferring to use a _pastry blender_, a couple of knives or forks, or even a food processor (a technique that requires mastery). When using your hands, be careful to pinch the chunks with your fingertips—not big, hot palms.

Kneading

This method is used mainly in yeast dough production. The idea is to agitate the gluten proteins within the flour, which creates the elastic texture needed to trap the gases of fermentation and allow the dough to rise.

There are several methods of kneading, including folding, rolling, slapping, and pounding the dough. But there is not one "right way" as long as the dough is getting a good workout. Work on a lightly floured surface with lightly floured hands, and push, fold, and roll the dough across the counter for 8 to 10 minutes. Avoid adding excess flour because it will make the dough harder to knead. The dough will change appearance, from a sticky, lumpy mass to a smooth, silky, firm dough.

Kneading by hand is easy, but it also can be done in an electric mixer (and in some recipes, even with a food processor). When using appliances, be sure the dough is actually slapping around the bowl and is not just clinging to the center hook or paddle and spinning around.

The Least You Need to Know

- Whenever possible, use the ingredients recommended in the recipes.
- Some substitutions have little effect while others can drastically change the outcome.
- Proper techniques produce the best possible finished products.

Chapter 2

Baking and Pans

In This Chapter

- Stocking the basic pans for snack cakes
- Adjusting recipes to suit a variety of pans
- Understanding your oven

Once you have the batter made, you need to bake it in something. This is an important step, but it shouldn't be intimidating. There is no reason to go out and buy hundreds of dollars worth of equipment. A few basic pieces will suffice. Then again, if you're the gadgety type, there are dozens of specialty pans just waiting to be added to your cookware inventory.

The Basics

There are a few essentials you cannot do without in the realm of snack baking. When stocking your kitchen with equipment, start with the following pieces.

Baking Sheets

Also known as cookie sheets or sheet pans, these are flat metal trays generally measuring around 12x16 inches. Many varieties have a one-inch lip around the edge that allows it to double as a jelly roll pan. They are made from a variety of materials, but aluminum is by far the most common. It's a good choice, as it conducts heat evenly. Whatever pan you choose, look for something easy to wash with no special coatings that could be easily chipped or scrubbed off.

Regardless of the pan material, it should be coated in nonstick cooking spray before baking. Small scratches in a nonstick coating will cause sticking. If you have parchment paper, use it instead of the spray. It is naturally nonstick, easy to clean (just throw it away), and prolongs the life of your pans by eliminating the need to scrub them to death.

Muffin Tins

For cupcake production, muffin tins are essential. They come in all shapes and sizes, from miniature to gigantic. Recipes in this book are designed for a standard muffin tin with a capacity of four fluid ounces. Using another size is fine, but be sure to adjust the baking time and temperature (see below).

It is not a good idea to purchase muffin tins with more than a dozen cups, because the cakes will not bake evenly. The edges become overdone as you wait for the center cups to solidify. The best results come from six-cup pans.

Pans should be coated in spray and lined with paper cups. Be sure to spray the top surface of the pan, too, as batter can rise up and over—and you don't want the crowns to stick.

Baking Pans

Most recipes in this book call for 9×13 pans. This standard rectangular pan, usually about 2 inches deep, is often referred to as a *brownie* or *lasagna* pan. Other sizes work too, but the larger pans will require an increase in the recipe.

In days past, the more common size pan was an 8×8 square. This pan is fine to use, but be aware that the resulting product will be a bit thicker.

If you want to be precise about changing pans, you can measure its volume with water. A 9×13 pan filled $^1/_2$ to $^3/_4$ full holds between six and eight cups of batter. Measure the capacity of the pan you'd like to use with water to determine how much to increase or decrease your recipe.

Mini Loaf Pans

An entire chapter of this book is dedicated to little cakes made out of traditionally large cake recipes. To bake these in individual sizes, you'll need special pans. Most large supermarkets carry small foil pans, and fancy cookware stores generally sell aluminum, stainless, and iron varieties. You can also buy just about any shape pan you want on the Internet. See Appendix B for retail and Internet sources.

Mini Pie Pans

Pie and tart pans of all shapes and sizes are readily available in cookware stores and online. If you find yourself in a pinch, however, these recipes can be made in muffin tins by lining each cup with dough and filling according to the recipe. Paper liners are a good idea in this application to ease the tart's removal.

Silicone Pans

Silicone is a flexible, translucent polymer that is both liquid and solid. Contained within the fibers of parchment paper and used recently for all shapes and forms of bakeware, it can withstand temperatures in excess of 650°F.

Silicone first started showing up in bakeware in the late 1980s as plastic mats that made delicate sugar and pastry work quick and easy. Today, everything imaginable is made out of silicone, including baking sheets, muffin tins, bundt pans, and even hot pads.

Silicone baking pans are flexible, so they usually need another kind of pan for support in the oven. And because plastic is an insulator, baked goods do not always brown nicely. While they are easy to clean, they are not nonstick and should be prepared just as you would any other pan.

Paper Pans

Fancy European bakeries have used paper pans for decades. They make gift-giving a breeze. They are available in many shapes and sizes, in gourmet supply stores, and on the Internet (see Appendix B). Prepare them as you would a metal pan.

Adding Heat

Oven temperatures are determined by the size of an item and the ingredients it contains. Any batter can be baked in any size pan as long as you make the necessary time and temperature adjustments. There are a few general rules you should follow if you decide to alter the size or shape of a recipe.

Temperature

Most recipes designate a specific pan, but you can bake cakes in any size pan—from cupcake size to sheet cake size and beyond. Smaller pans will bake faster and should be baked at a higher temperature for the best structure—usually around 25° hotter than when the indicated pan is large.

Large cakes benefit from a cooler oven (at least, toward the end of baking). Monitor the cooking process carefully. It takes the heat longer to enter the center of a large cake than a small one. If the temperature is too high, the outer crust will overcook and can even burn before the center of the cake has begun to solidify. Adjust the temperature at least 25° lower than when the indicated pan is smaller.

Helpful Hints

Larger pans will, of course, need more batter. The recipes can simply be multiplied as necessary. Keep the size of your mixers and bowls in mind when increasing recipes, though. Large recipes are sometimes hard to mix thoroughly. It is better to make a batter twice than to wrestle with an overflowing mixer bowl.

Ovens

Everyone's oven bakes differently. Most have a hot spot, or a corner that holds more heat and cooks faster than the rest of the oven. If you bake a lot, you know where your hot spot is. If not, check the browning periodically throughout the baking process. If you see one edge getting brown quickly, rotate the pan. If more than one pan is in the oven, rotate their positions—switching left to right, top to bottom or back to front.

Both gas and electric ovens cook equally well. Gas stovetops are preferable, though, as the heat is more easily controlled.

Helpful Hints

Beware! When rotating pans in the oven, it is important to move quickly. Reach in and slide things around as best you can while keeping the pans in the oven. Removing the pans from the oven, even briefly, will cause a drop in temperature that can cause a collapse.

Convection ovens have a fan that makes the oven hotter, which is useful when you want something to cook fast. They were originally developed with the belief that a fan circulating the air would brown food evenly. Unfortunately, it didn't work. Things still brown unevenly with the fan, and it is still necessary to rotate pans throughout baking.

Convection works well for cookies, biscuits, muffins, puff pastry, and other small stuff. Larger items will brown on the outside and look done before they are done on the inside. It is terrible for large loaves of bread, pound cakes, white meringues, or anything that's delicate (like custards). For avid bakers, convection ovens are only useful if the fan can be disabled or you have another traditional, still-air oven.

Baking Times

Baking times are always given in recipes, but they should never be considered 100 percent accurate. Variations in ovens, pans, ingredients, and the number of items baking in the oven make all baking times approximate.

To be sure you know when to remove your items from the oven, use your eyes and your common sense. If the time is up but it doesn't look done, there is nothing wrong with baking longer. And to be sure you do not overbake an item, get in the habit of checking it halfway through the indicated time. The oven temperature, batter consistency, pan size, and type of metal it's made from can completely alter the baking time.

Judging Doneness

The most common method of testing a cake is by inserting a pick into its center. If it comes out clean (no crumbs), the cake is done. If there is wet batter stuck to the pick, it needs to be baked longer. Unfortunately, this is not an accurate test for all recipes. It doesn't work for gooey cakes and cakes with lots of add-ins, which will always produce a wet pick even when overbaked. Foam-based cakes will produce a clean pick before they are completely done.

So … how do you judge the doneness of a cake? The best test is touch. Gently press the top center of the cake with your finger. If it leaves an indentation, the cake is not ready. If it springs back to the touch, it's done.

Another good indication of doneness is the cake's edge. As proteins solidify within the batter, the entire cake contracts. A finished cake, if baked in a greased pan, will have a small gap between the crust and the pan.

Coloration is another good indicator. Golden brown is the goal, although with chocolate batters that is hard to determine. Small or thin cakes, however, should be pulled from the oven when still fairly blonde because they can become cracker-crisp if allowed to brown. This is especially important if you are making jelly roll or petit-four cakes that need to be rolled or cut.

The Least You Need to Know

- ◆ Cake can be baked in any size pan as long as you adjust the time and temperature accordingly.

- ◆ Large cakes need to bake at lower temperatures than small cakes.

- ◆ Do not rely on the written baking time. Use your eyes and common sense to judge doneness.

Chapter 3

Frostings, Fillings, and Toppings

In This Chapter

- ◆ Properly working with chocolate, sugar, and cream
- ◆ Frosting and filling recipes for every occasion
- ◆ Inspiring your creativity with variations on basic recipes

Before you dive into these finishing touches, there are a few techniques you should read about. Understanding the nuances of chocolate, sugar, and cream will help you avoid unpleasant outcomes.

Chocolate

The chocolate recipes in this book call mainly for chocolate chips. I like using chips because they are easy to find and melt quickly. The flavor of most chocolate chips, however, is unremarkable. If you long for a more refined chocolate, feel free to make a substitution. Just be sure to use the type of chocolate called for in the recipe (bittersweet in most cases). Milk and white chocolates have more fat and do not work properly unless adjustments to the recipe are made. If you use a bar of chocolate, be sure to chop your chocolate into pieces roughly the same size as a chocolate chip for even melting.

Melting chocolate is not hard, but it can be temperamental. Most recipes call for it to be melted with butter in a saucepan over low heat. Care must be taken to stir continuously, because chocolate can burn easily. If chocolate is to be melted alone, it is usually done over a *water bath* or *double boiler*. You can rig up your own water bath by placing a bowl over a simmering pot of water. Stir the chocolate frequently, and when it is nearly melted turn off the heat and let it sit and finish melting. Try not to get any water in the bowl of chocolate, because even a small drop will cause the chocolate to clump or seize.

Chocolate can be melted in the microwave, too, but it takes constant monitoring and stirring. Never cook chocolate in a microwave for more than 15 seconds or it will burn in patches. Put the chocolate in a glass or ceramic bowl, and heat it in 1- to 15-second intervals—stirring in between.

> **Sweet Talk**
>
> A **water bath** or **double boiler** is a technique designed to apply gentle heat. The food is suspended in a bowl 1-2 inches above simmering water, providing indirect heat, which is less likely to scorch or burn. In French, it is called a bain-marie.

Sugar

Many cooks avoid cooking sugar because they are worried about crystallization, an event that can ruin a batch of sugar within minutes. Sugar starts out in crystalline form. Once liquefied, the two single sugar molecules—glucose and fructose— separate. During cooking, they naturally try to rejoin with each other. If a stray crystal or a speck of anything foreign enters the pot, the molecules will gravitate towards it, grab hold, and start forming a gigantic crystal. It's the phenomenon demonstrated when you made rock candy in science class.

To prevent those pesky molecules from taking over, recipes contain extra glucose (in the form of corn syrup) or acid. These ingredients discourage the reforming of crystals. There are also some precautions you can take while the sugar is cooking. Never stir a pot of sugar unless a recipe tells you to. (It will when there are other ingredients in the pot, like butter.) Such agitation will bring any foreign particles into play. If crystals begin to accumulate on the side of the pan as the sugar cooks, they can be dissolved and wiped away with a moist, clean pastry brush. Be careful not to simply wash the crystals down into the pot.

The best defense against crystallization is simply to use a clean pot, clean sugar, and wipe the sides of the pot clean of any stray grains of sugar before the pot hits the heat. Set the pot over high heat, and do not touch it until it is done. The more you wiggle, stir, shake, and jostle the syrup, the closer to the edge of crystallization you push it.

When cooking sugar on top of the stove, a candy thermometer makes the task super simple (provided that the thermometer is accurate). The old-fashioned method of testing sugar stages with ice water is easy, too, and in most cases more reliable. Have a bowl of ice water ready. As the sugar cooks, the bubbles get larger and the mixture starts to thicken. Spoon out a small amount of the sugar into the ice water, and immediately feel its consistency. If the recipe calls for soft-ball sugar, you should easily be able to form the sugar into a ball with your fingers. Hard-ball sugar will keep the ball shape once formed. At the crack stage, it will harden immediately once it hits the water and will crack easily.

Sugar boiled on its own will be clear until it reaches the crack stage, when it begins turning amber as it hits caramel, and on to black as it starts to burn. If the recipe has other ingredients, like butter or milk, it will begin to darken sooner. Hard-crack stage will always be a rich caramel color.

Whipped Egg White Meringue

Some recipes in this chapter and throughout the book call for an egg white meringue. When whipping egg whites, there are a couple of rules to follow. The bowl and the whip must be clean. Any speck of fat in the mix will inhibit the whites from taking in air. Egg yolks are full of fat and are a common culprit. When separating the eggs, don't let any yolk into the white bowl. The smallest amount can drastically reduce the amount of air that an egg white can hold.

Some recipes call for a simple, or *common* meringue, with raw egg whites whipped until they are stiff and granulated sugar sprinkled in at the medium or stiff peak stage. This is an unstable method, so it is important to stop the whipping at the appropriate time. To judge the peak stage, spoon a bit of meringue out of the bowl and hold it upright. If it makes a peak that stands erect at the tip of the spoon, it is a *stiff peak*. If the peak bends over a bit at the tip, it is a *medium peak*. If the peak flops all the way over, it is a *soft peak*.

Some of the recipes call for sugar syrup to be poured into the whipping whites. Seven-Minute Icing, found in this chapter, is a good example. It is important to cook the sugar to the proper stage. Use a candy thermometer or the traditional ice water test for best results.

Once the syrup is ready, pour it slowly into the whites as you whip. The movement is important to prevent the heat of the sugar from overcooking the eggs. If you do not have an electric mixer, get a friend to drizzle in the sugar while you whisk by hand. If you don't have a mixer or an extra set of hands nearby, you can secure the bowl of egg whites by placing it on a damp towel.

Custards

A couple of the recipes in this chapter are based on a stovetop egg custard. Careful cooking is important for proper texture and flavor. Overcooked custards have a curdled appearance and taste overwhelmingly of eggs.

Eggs contain protein. When protein is heated, it coagulates. The hotter it gets, the tighter it becomes. Using steak as an example, the texture is much softer when cooked rare than when well done. When cooking stovetop custards, stirring must remain constant to keep the eggs from settling on the bottom, where they will heat and solidify quickly. Remember that cookware remains hot even after it is removed from direct heat. Be sure to strain the finished custard quickly. Getting it out of the hot saucepan as soon as possible will prevent curdling.

Cream

When it comes to using cream, keep it cold until you are ready to whip it. If you need to whip your cream on a hot day, make sure to whip it over an *ice bath.*

There are several ways to whip cream. The easiest and probably fastest is to use a machine. When you use a stand or handheld electric mixer, keep your eye on it and be ready to stop the machine as soon as the proper stage is reached.

Sweet Talk

An **ice bath** refers to water used to quickly cool foods. Foods can be placed in directly, or set on top in another bowl, and stirred until cool.

If you decide to whip your cream by hand, use the largest whisk and bowl you can find. The more surface area your cream has, the faster it will whip. Be aware, especially if your arm tires easily, that speed is key. Be sure to whip in a circular motion and actually lift the whisk out of the cream with each pass. This method brings more air into the cream, speeding up the task.

Finally, as mentioned earlier, you don't want to overwhip the cream—so to judge the peak stages as you are whipping, periodically scoop out some cream and hold it upside down so the cream makes a peak. If the peak droops over, it is soft. If the peak droops just a little, it is medium. If the peak holds stiff and upright, it is stiff. However, if the peak looks like cottage cheese, you whipped it too much, made butter, and will have to start over.

Sweetened Whipped Cream

The French name for this all-purpose topping is crème chantilly. The flavor should be subtly sweet and not cloying because it is generally used to top desserts that are already sweetened. The flavor is easily changed to suit any recipe.

2 cups heavy whipping cream, well chilled

3 TB. sugar

1 tsp. vanilla extract

Makes 3 to 4 cups

Prep Time: 10 minutes

1. In a large bowl, combine cream, sugar, and vanilla. Using a whisk or an electric mixer, whip cream until soft peaks appear. Watch carefully as the cream continues to stiffen, and stop when it reaches medium peaks.

2. Use immediately or chill for up to 30 minutes.

Variations

- ◆ **Chocolate Cream:** Melt 1 cup chocolate chips over a water bath or in a microwave and allow to cool to lukewarm. By hand, whisk cooled melted chocolate into soft-peak cream until just combined. Be careful not to overwhip.

- ◆ **Coffee Cream:** By hand, whisk coffee extract (or 1 tablespoon espresso powder mixed with 1 tablespoon water) into soft-peak cream until just combined. Be careful not to overwhip.

- ◆ **Coconut Cream:** Drain the liquid from a 15-ounce can of coconut milk. By hand, whisk thick coconut paste into soft-peak cream until just combined. Be careful not to overwhip. Coconut extract also can be used in place of vanilla.

Helpful Hints

Canned coconut milk is not really milk but is grated coconut meat that is pressed to remove all the liquid. The liquid found naturally in the center of the coconut is called coconut water (or coconut liquor).

Coconut milk in the can is full of oil, which separates from the water of the nut and sinks to the bottom of the can. This makes separating the fat from the water easy. Be sure not to shake the can. And remember to save the drained water for another use, like smoothies, piña coladas, or coconut rice.

White Glaze

This glaze is perfect for doughnuts, cookies, petit fours, sweet rolls, or anything you think deserves a little shine. It is thin, translucent, and just sweet enough.

⅓ cup unsalted butter

2 cups powdered sugar, sifted

1½ tsp. vanilla extract

¼ tsp. kosher salt

¼-½ cup hot water

Makes 3 to 4 cups
Prep Time: 10 minutes
Cook Time: 15 minutes

1. Melt butter in a large saucepan over medium heat.

2. Off heat, stir in powdered sugar and vanilla until smooth.

3. Add salt and adjust consistency with hot water, 1 tablespoon at a time, as needed. Use while hot.

Variations

◆ Additional liquid flavoring can be added in place of vanilla. Food coloring also should be added at this time.

Helpful Hints

Be sure to add food coloring slowly, one drop at a time. If the color is too light, it's easy to add more. But if it's too dark, you can't take it out!

Chocolate Ganache

This classic recipe is the base of dozens of desserts. Chilled and rolled, it is the center of a truffle. Poured hot over cakes, it is a shiny glaze. Whipped stiff, it makes a pretty frosting. Allowed to set naturally, it is the perfect filling.

8 oz. (8 squares or 1½ cup chips) bitter-sweet chocolate

1 cup heavy cream

Makes about 2 cups

Prep Time: 5 minutes

Cook Time: 15 minutes

1. In a small saucepan over high heat, bring cream to a boil.
2. Place chocolate in a medium-size bowl. When boiling, pour cream over chocolate, let stand 3 to 5 minutes, then whisk until smooth.

Variations

- ◆ **Glaze:** Use immediately.

- ◆ **Room Temperature:** Let stand at room temperature overnight (at least 6 hours) until set. Ganache should be spreadable but not runny.

- ◆ **Whipped:** Let glaze cool to room temperature, then whip just until soft peaks form. Be careful not to overwhip.

- ◆ **Milk Chocolate:** Use milk chocolate and adjust recipe to 16 ounces milk chocolate and 1 cup heavy cream.

- ◆ **White Chocolate:** Use white chocolate and adjust recipe to 1½ pound (24 ounces) white chocolate and 1 cup heavy cream.

Streusel

2 cups all-purpose flour

1 cup unsalted butter, chilled and diced

1 cup sugar

Makes about 4 cups

Prep Time: 10 minutes

Cook Time: See individual recipes

1. In a large bowl, combine flour and sugar. Mix well, then cut in butter, using fingertips or a pastry blender, until chunks are pea-sized.

2. The streusel is ready if it holds together when squeezed but easily crumbles apart. Be careful not to overmix or the streusel will become gummy.

3. Generously crumble streusel on top of the item to be baked, and proceed as directed. Store leftover streusel in the freezer for up to one month.

Helpful Hints

Streusel is also known as *crisp, crumb,* and *crumble*. It is an easy thing to whip up, and it keeps for weeks in the freezer. So make a big batch and have it on hand to top your muffins, coffee cakes, and pies.

Variations

◆ Streusel can be made with brown sugar, white sugar, or a combination.

◆ You can add up to 1 cup of finely chopped nuts of your choice, 1 cup of rolled oats, and 1 to 2 tablespoons of your favorite spices.

Chocolate Fudge Frosting

This is a good all-purpose chocolate frosting recipe. It's not too sweet, but it is very chocolaty. Don't make this frosting until the cake has cooled. If it sits around, it will firm up and be very hard to spread. If this happens, place the bowl of icing over a pan of simmering water and stir until it softens.

$\frac{1}{2}$ cup brown sugar

$\frac{1}{4}$ cup water

2 TB. corn syrup

$1\frac{1}{2}$ cups chocolate chips

3 TB. butter, softened

1 TB. vanilla extract

1-lb. box powdered sugar, sifted

2 TB. hot water

Makes about 4 cups
Prep Time: 10 minutes
Cook Time: 20 minutes

1. Combine sugar, water, and corn syrup in a large saucepan and bring to a boil over high heat. When sugar is dissolved, remove from heat, add chocolate chips, butter, and vanilla, and stir to melt.

2. Add powdered sugar alternately with hot water. Adjust frosting consistency with more hot water or powdered sugar as needed. Frost cake immediately.

Variations

◆ **Mocha Frosting:** Replace the water with an equal amount of strong brewed coffee or espresso.

◆ **Chocolate-Mint Frosting:** Add 1 teaspoon peppermint extract or 2 to 3 drops of peppermint oil in place of the vanilla.

◆ **Chocolate-Orange Frosting:** Replace the water with an equal amount of Grand Marnier liqueur. For a nonalcoholic version, use thawed orange juice concentrate.

Chocolate Sour Cream Frosting

This chocolate frosting has a slight tang thanks to the addition of sour cream. It's perfect for desserts that are already very sweet.

1 cup chocolate chips

4 TB. (1/2 stick) softened butter

1/2 cup sour cream

1 TB. vanilla extract

1 (1-lb.) box powdered sugar, sifted

2-4 TB. hot water

Makes about 4 cups

Prep Time: 10 minutes

Cook Time: 20 minutes

1. Melt together chocolate and butter in a double boiler or a bowl set over simmering water. Stir in sour cream and vanilla.

2. Add sugar alternately with water. Adjust frosting consistency with more hot water or powdered sugar as needed. Spread evenly over cooled cake.

Vanilla Frosting

This sweet icing has a wonderful texture, perfect for spreading and piping.

12 oz. (2 sticks) butter, softened

2 TB. vanilla extract

3 1/2 cups powdered sugar, sifted

1/4 cup heavy whipping cream

Makes about 5 cups

Prep Time: 10 minutes

Cook Time: 20 minutes

1. Cream butter in a large bowl with a sturdy spoon or electric mixer until smooth and lump free. Add vanilla.

2. Slowly add half the powdered sugar, beating until light and fluffy. Add half the cream and mix well. Add remaining sugar and beat until fluffy.

Vanilla Custard

The French name for this recipe is *crème pâtissière*, and it is standard in bake shops and pastry kitchens around the world. You may recognize it as vanilla pudding.

4 egg yolks

1 cup sugar

⅓ cup cornstarch

4 cups half-and-half

2 TB. vanilla extract

2 TB. butter

> **Makes about 4 cups**
> **Prep Time:** 10 minutes
> **Cook Time:** 20 minutes

1. In a small bowl, whisk together egg yolks, sugar, and cornstarch and set aside.

2. In a large saucepan, combine half-and-half and vanilla and bring to a boil over high heat.

3. While boiling, ladle ½ cup of hot half-and-half into yolks and whisk quickly to combine. Pour the warmed yolks into the saucepan, and over high heat whisk immediately and vigorously until mixture begins to resemble thick sour cream (about 2 minutes).

4. Remove from heat, add butter, and stir to combine. Pour immediately into a clean bowl and cover with plastic wrap pressed directly on the surface.

5. Cool to room temperature, then refrigerate at least one hour before use.

Variations

◆ **Super-Vanilla:** For an exquisite vanilla flavor, use a vanilla bean. Slice it in half lengthwise and scrape the tiny seeds into the pot. Add the pod, too, for extra flavor, and strain it out before use.

Tidbits

The name of the technique used here to combine the eggs into the hot liquid is tempering. By warming the yolks ever so slightly before stirring them into the pot, you will avoid a pan full of scrambled eggs. Be sure to stir continuously once everything is combined.

Seven-Minute Icing

This recipe is also known as *Italian meringue, white mountain icing,* and *boiled icing.* Fluffy and light, it is an important element in many classic French pastries, meringue pies, and Baked Alaska.

1 cup sugar

½ cup light corn syrup

¼ cup water

½ tsp. kosher salt

4 egg whites

1 tsp. vanilla extract

Makes about 5 cups

Prep Time: 20 minutes

Cook Time: 20 minutes

1. In a large saucepan, combine sugar, corn syrup, water, and salt. Bring to a boil and cook over high heat until it reaches firm ball stage (245°F).

2. Meanwhile, in a large bowl using a whisk or an electric mixer, whip egg whites to stiff peaks. Continue whipping while slowly drizzling in sugar syrup. Add vanilla and whip until stiff peaks are formed.

Variations

◆ **Chocolate:** For a dark or milk chocolate icing, slowly drizzle one cup of melted chocolate into the whites during the last few minutes of whipping.

Heads Up

When adding the sugar syrup, try not to drizzle it on the whipping whisk. This tends to spin it into threads like cotton candy. And don't be alarmed as the addition of sugar syrup deflates your stiff whites. Continued whisking brings the peaks back.

Coconut Pecan Frosting

This is the classic filling for German Chocolate Cake, but its use is not limited to that recipe. It goes well with spice cakes, fruitcakes, and makes a great bar cookie topping.

$\frac{3}{4}$ cup evaporated milk

1 cup brown sugar

$\frac{1}{2}$ cup unsalted butter

1 tsp. vanilla

3 egg yolks

$1\frac{1}{2}$ cups shredded coconut

1 cup pecans, chopped

Makes about 4 cups

Prep Time: 20 minutes

Cook Time: 20 minutes

1. Crack yolks into a small bowl and set aside.

2. Combine milk, sugar, butter, and vanilla in a large saucepan over high heat and stir until it reaches a boil. While boiling, ladle $\frac{1}{2}$ cup into yolks and whisk quickly to combine.

3. Pour the warmed yolks back into the saucepan, and over high heat whisk immediately and vigorously until mixture thickens.

4. Remove from heat and stir in coconut and pecans. Stir periodically as the mixture cools. Cool completely.

Caramel Sauce

Here is another must-have pastry recipe. It will keep for weeks in the refrigerator and can be embellished to suit your mood.

2 cups sugar

¼ cup water

1 TB. lemon juice

1½ cups cream

2 oz. (½ stick) unsalted butter

Makes about 4 cups
Prep Time: 5 minutes
Cook Time: 30 minutes

1. In a large saucepan, combine sugar and water. Mix together well, wipe all stray sugar crystals off the sides of the pan, and place over high heat. Cook without moving or stirring.

2. When the mixture reaches a rolling boil, pour lemon juice into the center of the pot. Do not stir. Continue cooking until sugar is a dark, golden amber color.

3. Remove from heat and carefully whisk in cream. Add butter, whisk until smooth, then cool to room temperature.

Variations

◆ Any number of flavor additions can be made after the caramel sauce is complete. Try adding vanilla, espresso, peanut butter, or melted chocolate.

Heads Up

When the cream is added to the caramel, it will erupt like a volcano. Stand back, and watch out for the steam. Stirring will cool it and calm it down. If there are lumps after the cream is added, take it back to the stove and stir it over low heat until the lumps dissolve.

Chocolate Custard

This is a classic version of chocolate pudding. Creamy and rich, it can be used to fill hundreds of different pastries. It's not bad on its own, either.

4 egg yolks

1 cup sugar

⅓ cup cornstarch

4 cups half-and-half

1 TB. vanilla extract

2 oz. bittersweet chocolate

2 TB. butter

Makes about 4 cups
Prep Time: 10 minutes
Cook Time: 20 minutes

1. In a small bowl, whisk together egg yolks, sugar, and cornstarch and set aside.

2. In a large saucepan, combine half-and-half and vanilla and bring to a boil over high heat. While boiling, ladle ½ cup of hot half-and-half into yolks and whisk quickly to combine.

3. Pour the warmed yolks into the saucepan, and over high heat whisk immediately and vigorously until mixture begins to resemble thick sour cream (about 2 minutes).

4. Remove from heat, add chocolate and butter, and stir to combine. Pour immediately into a clean bowl and cover with plastic wrap pressed directly on the surface.

5. Cool to room temperature, then refrigerate at least one hour before use.

Heads Up _____

Don't make this recipe with milk chocolate. The light brown color combined with the deep-yellow yolks of the eggs turns this custard's color into an unappealing gray.

Lemon Curd

This recipe can be used as a filling or topping for pastry—or, as it was originally intended, a spread for toast and scones.

6 whole eggs

5 egg yolks, reserving the whites

1¾ cups sugar

Zest of 4 lemons

1⅓ cups lemon juice

1 cup (2 sticks) butter

Makes 3-4 cups
Prep time: 10 minutes
Cook time: 15 minutes

1. In a large saucepan, combine whole eggs, yolks, sugar, lemon zest and juice, salt, and butter. Mix well and set over high heat. Stir continuously until mixture thickens to sour cream consistency.

2. Strain immediately through a fine wire mesh strainer into a clean bowl and cover with plastic wrap pressed directly on the surface.

3. Cool to room temperature, then refrigerate at least one hour before use.

Cream Cheese Frosting

2 oz. (½ stick) butter, softened

1 (8-oz.) package cream cheese, softened

1 TB. vanilla

¼ tsp. kosher salt

1 (1-lb.) box powdered sugar, sifted

Makes about 4 cups
Prep Time: 15 minutes

1. Cream together butter and cream cheese with a sturdy spoon or electric mixer until lump-free.

2. Add vanilla and salt, then slowly add powdered sugar and mix until smooth.

Part 2

Cupcakes

No matter how serious a person you are, you can't help but smile when someone hands you a cupcake. They are the definition of fun food. Small enough to hold in your hand, stuffed with cream, frosted with sugar, or covered in sprinkles, cupcakes make life a little sweeter.

Cupcakes are nothing but baby cakes. Any cake recipe can become a cupcake. All you need is a muffin tin and the desire to be cute. And what cake wouldn't aspire to be cute?

These chapters include something for everyone, including miniaturized large cakes, stylish single servings, childhood favorites, and copycat creations.

Chapter 4

Filled Cupcakes

In This Chapter

◆ Cakes with baked-in fillings

◆ Fillings added to finished cakes

◆ Fun new flavor combinations and classic favorites

The only thing that is more fun than eating a cupcake is eating a cupcake with filling. Just when you think things couldn't get any better, you take a bite, and bam! You hit filling. Oh, the joy!

The Mechanics of Filling

Fillings can be added in a number of ways. Some—such as whole berries, sliced fruit, or chunky chocolate and nuts—are baked into the center of the cake. Others, like delicate creams and custards, must be added when the cakes are cooked and cooled.

To add fillings after baking, the cake can either be hollowed out and filled by hand or injected with the help of a pastry bag. Hollowing out a cake involves nothing more than a little chiseling and sculpting. Injecting filling is closer to the technique used in mass-produced snack cakes.

Pastry bags are the easiest way to inject filling. They are available in most cookware, cake supply, and craft stores and even in some super-markets. Tips come in a number of shapes and sizes, but nothing fancy is needed here. Snip off the point of your bag, slide the tip inside, and push it down into the opening you just made.

When working with a pastry bag, always fold down a large cuff at the top before filling. This makes reloading much neater. Try not to fill the bag more than half full. If you do, the filling is likely to ooze out the wrong end as you pipe.

If a pastry bag is not in your future, a plastic storage bag—preferably with a zipper—works just as well. Fill it half full and snip off the corner.

Chocolate-Covered Banana Cupcakes

If you love chocolate-covered bananas and cupcakes, then this is your lucky day! This moist banana cake covered in rich chocolate packs a banana surprise inside. Calling all monkeys!

2 oz. (½ stick) unsalted butter

¾ cup sugar

6 ripe bananas, divided

1 egg

¼ cup sour cream

2 cups all-purpose flour

1½ tsp. baking powder

½ tsp. kosher salt

1 cup chocolate chips

1 recipe Chocolate Ganache, room temperature (see Chapter 3)

1 cup banana chips

1 cup chopped peanuts or almonds

Makes 12 cupcakes
Prep Time: 30 minutes
Cook Time: 30 minutes
Finishing Time: 30 minutes

1. Preheat the oven to 350°F. Coat a muffin tin with nonstick cooking spray, and insert paper cups.

2. In a large bowl, beat together butter and sugar until creamy and smooth. Add three bananas and egg and beat until creamy. Stir in sour cream.

3. Sift together flour, baking powder, and salt and slowly stir into batter. Fold in chocolate chips.

4. Fill muffin cups half full with batter. Slice remaining bananas into wheels and add three to four to each cup. Top with remaining batter so that the muffin tins are filled to the rim.

5. Bake for 20 to 30 minutes until firm to the touch. Cool completely.

6. Frost with ganache and top with banana chips and nuts.

Black Forest Cupcakes

Black Forest Cake is a classic creation known in Germany as Schwarz-wälder Kirschtorte. It traditionally oozes with kirschwasser, a double-distilled brandy made from the juice of black cherries. If you'd like a more kid-friendly version, replace the kirsch with two teaspoons of vanilla.

1 (15-oz.) can tart Montmorency cherries, drained

¼ cup kirsch

¾ cup water

¾ cup semisweet chocolate chips

8 oz. (2 sticks) unsalted butter

1 cup brown sugar

3 eggs

4¼ cups cake flour

1½ tsp. baking soda

½ tsp. baking powder

¼ tsp. kosher salt

⅔ cup sour cream

1 recipe Sweetened Whipped Cream (see Chapter 3)

1 TB. sugar

Chocolate shavings to decorate

Makes 12 cupcakes
Prep Time: 30 minutes
Cook Time: 30 minutes
Finishing Time: 30 minutes

1. Preheat the oven to 350°F. Coat a muffin tin with nonstick cooking spray, and insert paper cups.

2. Combine drained cherries with kirsch and set aside.

3. In a small saucepan, combine water and chocolate chips. Place over high heat and bring to a boil, stirring until melted. Remove from heat and cool.

4. In a large bowl, beat together butter and brown sugar until creamy and smooth. Add eggs one at a time, then add cooled chocolate and combine thoroughly.

5. Sift together cake flour, baking soda, baking powder, and salt and add alternately with sour cream.

6. Fill muffin cups half full with batter and add three to four cherries to each cup, reserving liquid and remaining cherries. Top with remaining batter so that the muffin tins are filled to the rim.

7. Bake for 20 to 30 minutes until firm to the touch. Cool completely.

8. Drizzle cherry liquid on top of each cupcake, letting it soak in. Ice with whipped cream and decorate with chocolate shavings and remaining cherries. Keep refrigerated until ready to serve.

Chocolate Turtle Cupcakes

Turtles are caramel-pecan candies dipped in chocolate. These cupcakes are as gooey as those candies—with an extra treat hidden in the center.

2 cups all-purpose flour

2 cups sugar

1 tsp. baking soda

½ cup unsalted butter

½ cup vegetable oil

1 cup water

¼ cup chocolate syrup

⅓ cup sour cream

2 eggs

1 tsp. vanilla extract

1 cup pecans

1 cup caramel sauce

1 cup chocolate chips

| **Makes 12 cupcakes** |
| **Prep Time:** 20 minutes |
| **Cook Time:** 30 minutes |

1. Preheat the oven to 350°F. Coat a muffin tin with nonstick cooking spray, and insert paper cups.

2. In a small bowl, sift together flour, baking soda, and salt and set aside.

3. In a large saucepan, combine butter, oil, water, and chocolate syrup and bring to a boil over high heat. Remove from heat, stir in flour mixture, sour cream, eggs, and vanilla and beat until smooth.

4. Fill muffin cups half full with batter and bake for 5 minutes until the surface begins to set.

5. Remove from oven and place one tablespoon of caramel sauce, two to three pecans, and five to six chocolate chips into each cup. Top with remaining batter so that the muffin tins are ¾ filled, then top each with more caramel sauce, pecans, and chocolate chips.

6. Return to the oven and bake another 10 to 15 minutes until firm to the touch. Cool completely.

Roasted Marshmallow Cupcakes

When you're longing for the great outdoors, this recipe takes the cake. The broiler provides the roasty, toasty flavor typically reserved for the campfire.

2 cups all-purpose flour

1 TB. baking powder

½ tsp. kosher salt

½ cup shortening

1 cup sugar

4 egg whites

1 TB. vanilla extract

½ cup evaporated milk

2 cups marshmallow creme

1 recipe Seven-Minute Icing (see Chapter 3)

Makes 12 cupcakes
Prep Time: 20 minutes
Cook Time: 30 minutes
Finishing Time: 20 minutes

1. Preheat the oven to 350°F. Coat a muffin tin with nonstick cooking spray, and insert paper cups.

2. Beat shortening and sugar together until smooth; set aside.

3. Whip egg whites to stiff peaks and set aside.

4. Combine milk and vanilla extract.

5. In a small bowl, sift together flour, baking powder, and salt and add alternately to shortening mixture with milk. Lighten batter with ⅓ of the egg whites, then fold in remaining whites until just combined.

6. Fill muffin cups half full with batter. Add one to two tablespoons of marshmallow creme to each cup. Top with remaining batter so that the muffin tins are filled to the rim.

7. Bake for 20 to 30 minutes until firm to the touch. Cool completely.

8. Frost with Seven-Minute Icing, and arrange on a baking sheet. Place under the broiler for two to three minutes until icing is slightly browned.

Tidbits

If you live on the East Coast, your marshmallow creme goes by the name *fluff.*

Orange Dreamsicle Cupcakes

There is nothing quite as redolent of childhood as the flavors of orange and vanilla. The taste of these cakes will remind you of the neighborhood ice cream truck.

½ cup (2 sticks) unsalted butter

1 cup sugar

Zest and juice of 3 oranges, separated

2 eggs

2 cups cake flour

1 tsp. baking soda

½ tsp. kosher salt

⅔ cup sour cream

1 tsp. vanilla extract

½ recipe Vanilla Custard (see Chapter 3)

1 cup whipped topping

1 recipe Vanilla Frosting (see Chapter 3)

1 tsp. orange extract

Orange food color

Candy orange slices

Makes 12 cupcakes
Prep Time: 20 minutes
Cook Time: 30 minutes
Finishing Time: 30 minutes

1. Preheat the oven to 350°F. Coat a muffin tin with nonstick cooking spray, and insert paper cups.

2. In a large bowl, beat together butter, sugar, and orange zest until creamy and smooth. Add eggs one by one.

3. Sift together flour, baking soda, and salt and add alternately with sour cream. Stir in vanilla.

4. Fill muffin cups ¾ full with batter and bake for 20 to 30 minutes until firm to the touch. Cool completely.

5. Using a spoon, dig into the top center of the cake and hollow out the center, being careful to keep the removed cake in one piece.

6. Stir together Vanilla Custard and whipped topping, and spoon one to two tablespoons into the middle of the cakes. Replace the cake top, pushing it down to lay flush with the top of the cake.

7. Stir reserved orange juice, orange extract, and orange food color into Vanilla Frosting and frost cakes. Decorate with candy orange slices.

Classic Cream-Filled Chocolate Cupcakes

5 oz. unsweetened baking chocolate, chopped

$\frac{1}{2}$ cup honey

$\frac{1}{2}$ cup milk

4 egg yolks, divided

$\frac{1}{2}$ cup (1 stick) unsalted butter

1 cup sugar

$\frac{3}{4}$ cup heavy cream

1 tsp. vanilla extract

2 cups cake flour

1 tsp. baking soda

1 tsp. kosher salt

3 egg whites

1 recipe White Frosting, divided (see Chapter 3)

2 cups whipped topping

1 recipe Chocolate Ganache, warm (see Chapter 3)

Makes 12 cupcakes
Prep Time: 20 minutes
Cook Time: 30 minutes
Finishing Time: 20 minutes

1. Preheat the oven to 350°F. Coat muffin tins with nonstick cooking spray, and insert paper cups.

2. In a small saucepan over medium heat, combine chocolate, honey, and milk and stir until melted. Remove from heat and stir in two egg yolks; set aside.

3. Beat butter and sugar together until smooth. Add remaining egg yolks one by one, then stir in cooled chocolate mixture. Combine cream and vanilla extract; set aside. Sift together flour, baking powder, and salt and add to batter alternately with cream. Whip egg whites to stiff peaks and fold into batter.

4. Fill muffin cups ³/₄ full with batter and bake for 20 to 30 minutes until firm to the touch. Cool completely. Use a chopstick to make a hole in the top of each cake.

5. Combine ¹/₂ recipe of White Frosting with whipped topping. Using a small plain pastry tip, fill a pastry bag with frosting mixture. Insert the pastry tip into the center of each cake and inject a generous amount of cream. Dip the tops into liquid ganache and chill to set. Decorate with squiggles of remaining White Frosting, piped through a pastry bag fitted with a small plain tip.

Cream-Filled Yellow Cupcakes

These cakes are classically simple but fantastic. It is rumored that they can bring out the sunshine on a cloudy day.

½ cup (1 stick) unsalted butter

1 cup sugar

2 eggs

1½ cups buttermilk

1 TB. vanilla extract

1½ cups cake flour

1 TB. baking powder

½ tsp. kosher salt

4 cups Sweetened Whipped Cream (see Chapter 3)

> **Makes 12 cupcakes**
>
> **Prep Time:** 20 minutes
>
> **Cook Time:** 30 minutes
>
> **Finishing Time:** 20 minutes

1. Preheat the oven to 350°F. Coat muffin tins with nonstick cooking spray, and insert paper cups.

2. Beat butter and sugar together until smooth. Add eggs one by one.

3. Combine buttermilk and vanilla extract and set aside.

4. Sift together flour, baking powder, and salt and add buttermilk mixture alternately.

5. Fill muffin cups ¾ full with batter and bake for 20 to 30 minutes until firm to the touch. Cool completely.

6. Use a chopstick to make a hole in the top of each cake.

7. Using a small plain pastry tip, fill a pastry bag with Sweetened Whipped Cream. Insert the pastry tip into the center of each cake and inject a generous amount of cream.

8. Frost with more Sweetened Whipped Cream or dust with powdered sugar.

Chapter 5

Iced Cupcakes

In This Chapter

◆ Simple cupcake rules

◆ Funny, quirky cupcakes for kids of all ages

◆ Sophisticated cupcakes for alleged adults

Nothing says, "I care about you" more than an individual cake. It's the size that makes it special—big enough to celebrate and satisfy, yet small enough to avoid sharing. They are easy enough to make as long as you adhere to a few simple rules. Once you incorporate these rules into your recipes, you'll be ready to bake delicious cupcakes for young and old alike.

Cupcake Rules

Here are several important things to remember as you bake your treats.

First, if you have enough leftover batter for a few more cakes, fill the cups in the center of the muffin pan first. They will bake and brown more evenly than if you only fill the corner cups. And never fill empty muffin cups with water. The water gets hot and gives off steam … and both can burn you.

Cool cupcakes 5 to 10 minutes before you carefully remove them from the pan. If they are removed too soon, they can easily fall apart. If they are removed too late, there is a chance that they may stick. Wait until the pan is cool enough to touch but still warm. When you do take out the cupcakes, don't dump them upside down out of their pan—you will damage their beautiful tops.

You also will want to cool the cupcakes completely before frosting. If they are even a little warm, they will melt any frosting that contains fat (which is all of them).

Make it easy on yourself and bake cupcakes ahead. Unfrosted, they can be wrapped easily and kept at room temperature overnight or frozen for up to a week. Prepare the frosting ahead, too, but ice them just before serving for the neatest, freshest-looking cakes.

Finally, never bake cupcakes when you're hungry. It's a tummyache waiting to happen.

Coconut Cupcakes

White as Alaskan snow with the flavor of the tropics, this recipe is a favorite of adventurers everywhere. If you really want to jazz it up, add some chopped, toasted macadamia nuts.

2 cups all-purpose flour

1 TB. baking powder

½ tsp. kosher salt

½ cup shortening

1 cup sugar

4 egg whites

1 tsp. coconut extract

½ cup evaporated milk

1 recipe Seven-Minute Icing (see Chapter 3)

3 cups shredded coconut

Makes 12 cupcakes

Prep Time: 20 minutes

Cook Time: 25 minutes

Finishing Time: 30 minutes

1. Preheat the oven to 350°F. Coat a muffin tin with nonstick cooking spray, and insert paper cups.

2. Beat shortening and sugar together until smooth; set aside. Whip egg whites to stiff peaks and set aside. Combine milk and coconut extract.

3. In a small bowl, sift together flour, baking powder, and salt and add to shortening mixture alternately with milk. Lighten batter with ⅓ of the egg whites, then fold in remaining whites until just combined.

4. Transfer batter to prepared muffin tins, filling to the rim. Bake 25 minutes until firm and a pick inserted in the center comes out clean.

5. Cool completely, frost with Seven-Minute Icing, and decorate with shredded coconut.

Carrot Cupcakes

This is a moist, fruity cake that is sure to please. The cream cheese icing is standard fare but can easily be eliminated for a lighter treat.

2 cups all-purpose flour

2 tsp. baking powder

1½ tsp. baking soda

1 tsp. kosher salt

2 tsp. cinnamon

2 tsp. nutmeg

½ tsp. cloves

2 cups sugar

1½ cups vegetable oil

4 eggs

2 cups grated carrot

1 (8-oz.) can crushed pineapple with juice

1 cup chopped walnuts, divided

1 recipe Cream Cheese Frosting
(see Chapter 3)

> **Makes 8 to 10 cupcakes**
>
> **Prep Time:** 20 minutes
> **Cook Time:** 20 minutes
> **Finishing Time:** 20 minutes

1. Preheat the oven to 350°F. Coat a muffin tin with nonstick cooking spray, and insert paper cups.

2. Sift together flour, baking powder, baking soda, salt, cinnamon, nutmeg, and cloves and set aside.

3. In a large bowl, mix together oil, eggs, carrots, pineapple, and nuts. Slowly add the sifted ingredients, combine thoroughly, and fold in half the nuts.

4. Fill muffin cups ¾ full and bake 15 to 20 minutes until a pick inserted in the center of the cake comes out clean.

5. Cool completely, then frost with Cream Cheese Icing.

Chocolate Peppermint Stick Cupcakes

This holiday treat will keep your little angels smiling. If you can't wait for December, omit the peppermint and make them plain. Super dense and rich, these cupcakes will please your chocolate lovers all year long.

½ cup chocolate chips

½ cup (1 stick) unsalted butter

2 cups sugar

1 cup mayonnaise

2 eggs

½ cup milk

2 cups all-purpose flour

1 tsp. baking powder

1 tsp. baking soda

1 recipe Chocolate Ganache (see Chapter 3)

1 cup crushed candy canes

Makes 12 cupcakes
Prep Time: 20 minutes
Cook Time: 25 minutes
Finishing Time: 30 minutes

1. Preheat the oven to 350°F. Coat a muffin tin with nonstick cooking spray, and insert paper cups.

2. In a small saucepan over low heat, melt chocolate and butter together, stirring constantly. Remove from heat and stir in sugar, mayonnaise, and milk.

3. In a separate bowl, stir together flour, baking powder, and baking soda. Add melted chocolate mixture and beat together until well combined.

4. Transfer batter to prepared muffin tins, filling to the rim. Bake 25 minutes until firm and a pick inserted in the center comes out clean. Cool completely.

5. Frost each cake with two to three tablespoons ganache and a sprinkling of crushed candy canes.

Tidbits

Mayonnaise in a cake? This recipe is an old American classic, first popularized during World War II rationing when butter was scarce. Later, mayonnaise companies distributed such recipes as a way to boost sales.

German Chocolate Cupcakes

This recipe does not hail from Germany but was made in the mid-1800s with German sweet chocolate, which was developed by Sam German—an employee at Walter Baker & Co. (the manufacturer of the famous Baker's Chocolate).

¾ cup chocolate chips

½ cup boiling water

1 cup (2 sticks) unsalted butter

2 cups brown sugar

4 eggs, separated

2¼ cups all-purpose flour

1 tsp. baking soda

½ tsp. kosher salt

1 cup buttermilk

1 tsp. vanilla

1 recipe Coconut Pecan Frosting
(see Chapter 3)

Makes 24 cupcakes

Prep Time: 30 minutes

Cook Time: 20 minutes

Finishing Time:
30 minutes

1. Preheat the oven to 350°F. Coat a muffin tin with nonstick cooking spray, and insert paper cups.

2. Combine chocolate and water in a small saucepan over medium heat and stir until melted. Set aside.

3. In a large bowl, beat together butter and brown sugar until creamy and smooth. Add eggs one at a time, then add cooled chocolate and combine thoroughly.

4. Sift together flour, baking soda, and salt and add alternately with buttermilk.

5. Fill prepared muffin tins ¾ full with batter and bake 15 to 20 minutes until firm to the touch.

6. Cool completely and ice with Coconut Pecan Frosting.

Peanut Butter Cup Cupcakes

Chocolate and peanut butter is a favorite combination, but there are tons of alternatives that are equally as decadent. See the variations following the recipe for some ideas.

½ cup (1 stick) unsalted butter

1 tsp. baking powder

1 cup peanut butter

1 cup brown sugar, packed

3 eggs

1 tsp. vanilla

2⅓ cups all-purpose flour

1 cup whole milk

1 recipe Chocolate Ganache (see Chapter 3)

12 mini peanut butter cup candies

Makes 12 cupcakes
Prep Time: 20 minutes
Cook Time: 25 minutes
Finishing Time: 20 minutes

1. Preheat the oven to 350°F. Coat muffin tins with nonstick cooking spray, and insert paper cups.

2. Beat butter, peanut butter, and sugar together until smooth and creamy. Add eggs one at a time, then vanilla.

3. Sift together flour and baking powder and add alternately with milk.

4. Transfer batter to prepared muffin tins, filling to the rim. Bake 25 minutes until firm to the touch.

5. Cool completely. Frost each cupcake with two to three tablespoons ganache and top with a peanut butter cup.

Variations

◆ **Peanut Butter and Banana Cupcakes:** Add ½ cup peanut butter to a recipe of White Frosting (see Chapter 3) and garnish with banana chunks.

◆ **Peanut Butter and Jelly Cupcakes:** Top your cupcakes with Concord grape jam.

◆ **Fluffernutter Cupcakes:** Frost your cakes with marshmallow creme.

Pink Champagne Cupcakes

Nothing says "celebrate" like champagne. But why confine it to a glass? The addition of pink champagne to this cake recipe balances the sweetness with a delicately acidic tang. Add food coloring if you want to increase the pink factor.

⅔ cup shortening

1½ cups sugar

1-2 drops red food coloring (optional)

2¾ cups all-purpose flour

1 TB. baking powder

1 tsp. kosher salt

¾ cup pink champagne

6 egg whites, room temperature

1 recipe White Glaze (see Chapter 3)

> **Makes 12 cupcakes**
>
> **Prep Time:** 20 minutes
>
> **Cook Time:** 30 minutes
>
> **Finishing Time:**
> 20 minutes

1. Preheat the oven to 350°F. Coat muffin tins with nonstick cooking spray, and insert paper cups.

2. Beat shortening and sugar together until smooth and creamy. Add food coloring if desired.

3. Sift together flour, baking powder, and salt and add alternately with champagne.

4. Whip egg whites to stiff peaks. Lighten batter with ⅓ of the egg whites, then fold in remaining whites until just combined.

5. Transfer batter to prepared muffin tins, filling to the rim. Bake 25 minutes until firm to the touch.

6. Cool completely, then frost with warm White Glaze (tinted pink if desired).

Variations

◆ This recipe works well with liquor and is especially nice with both sherry and dark beer.

Red Velvet Cupcakes

This old-fashioned recipe from the Southern United States is deep, dark red (like Scarlett O'Hara's dress). The color is achieved by the addition of cocoa powder. Traditionally, this cake is paired with cream cheese frosting, but I also like to cover it with Seven-Minute Icing.

1½ cups sugar

1 cup vegetable oil

2 eggs

1 cup buttermilk

2 TB. cocoa powder

¼ cup red food coloring

2½ cups all-purpose flour

1 tsp. kosher salt

1 tsp. baking soda

1 TB. cider vinegar

1 recipe Cream Cheese Frosting
(see Chapter 3)

> **Makes about 24 cupcakes**
>
> **Prep Time:** 20 minutes
>
> **Cook Time:** 20 minutes
>
> **Finishing Time:** 30 minutes

1. Preheat the oven to 350°F. Coat a muffin tin with nonstick cooking spray, and insert paper cups.

2. In a large bowl, combine oil, sugar, eggs, and buttermilk.

3. In a separate bowl, combine cocoa and food coloring; mix well and add to batter. Sift together flour and salt and add to batter.

4. In a small bowl, combine baking soda and vinegar, mixing until foamy, and add immediately to batter. Stir just to combine.

5. Fill prepared muffin tins ¾ full with batter and bake 15 to 20 minutes until firm to the touch. Cool completely and ice with Cream Cheese Frosting.

Strawberry Shortcake Cupcakes

1 cup butter

2 cups sugar

5 eggs

1 tsp. vanilla

3 cups all-purpose flour

1 tsp. baking powder

¼ tsp. salt

1¼ cups milk

1 recipe Sweetened Whipped Cream
(see Chapter 3)

2 pints fresh strawberries, washed and
halved or sliced

Makes 12 cupcakes
Prep Time: 20 minutes
Cook Time: 25 minutes
Finishing Time: 15 minutes

1. Preheat the oven to 350°F. Coat muffin tins with nonstick cooking
    spray, and insert paper cups.

2. Beat butter and sugar together until smooth and creamy. Add eggs
    one at a time, then vanilla.

3. Sift together flour, baking powder, and salt and add alternately with
    milk.

4. Transfer batter to prepared muffin tins, filling ¾ full. Bake 25
    minutes or until firm to the touch. Cool completely, frost with
    Sweetened Whipped Cream, and decorate with fresh strawberries.

Variations

- ◆ **Peaches and Cream Cupcakes:** Replace strawberries with sweet,
  ripe peaches sliced in thin wedges.

- ◆ **Berries and Cream Cupcakes:** Use raspberries, blackberries,
  blueberries, or a combination in place of—or in addition to—the
  strawberries.

Part 3

Bars, Brownies, and Squares

What do you get when you cross a cookie and a cake? You get these chapters!

Bars, brownies, and squares are in a class by themselves. These recipes are at the heart of bake sales across America. They are easy to make, easy to serve, and oh so satisfying.

Bars are similar to cookies, but rather than being dropped on a baking sheet in individual portions, they are baked in a larger pan and cut into rectangles. Brownies are so named for their color and typically (although not always) refer to chocolate. Squares are often more cakelike than the other two—with or without toppings and icings.

Some recipes in this section are fancifully layered, iced, and decorated, while others are ready to eat as soon as they cool. The only criteria is that they are baked and cut from a rectangular pan. But throughout these chapters, you'll discover that even this rule can be fudged (sometimes literally).

Chapter 6

Bars

In This Chapter

- ◆ Simple rules for bars
- ◆ Lip-smacking bars to please the masses
- ◆ Sophisticated bars for the classy snacker

Some people may see the bar as a lazy man's cookie (an accusation that holds some truth). They certainly are easier to make than anything that must be baked individually.

The first bar cookies were indeed cookie dough that was simply spread out to fill a shallow baking pan. Baked like a cake then cut into small portions, bars were a welcome change of pace for busy homemakers of the early twentieth century. Today, however, bars have evolved to include some rather elaborate compositions.

Most bars have distinctive personalities and are generally more decadent than a cookie. They can get away with more gooeyness than a cookie ever could, and they often include more outrageous ingredients than a cookie would dare to dream of.

But with all their distinctive qualities, bars are not stuck up. They need no special treatment. They are simple, humble snacks that are welcome wherever treats are cherished.

Bar Rules

There are a couple things to remember to help ensure a successful bar result.

Be cool. It's important to let your bars cool completely before cutting them into serving pieces. Bars with a bottom crust are particularly prone to crumbling, and gooey bars will lose their filling if cut prematurely.

> **Sweet Talk**
>
> An **offset spatula** has a bend in its blade close to the handle. This allows you to spread batter in a pan right up to the edge.

Be neat. Use a wide *offset* metal spatula to remove your bars neatly from the pan. This tool is designed exactly for this purpose, and nothing else works as well.

Use moderation. These treats are richer than most cookies and can easily get you into trouble. Avoid a tummyache by slicing bars into small portions and serving them with plenty of milk to wash them down.

Butterfingers Peanut Butter Bars

If you are a fan of the Butterfinger candy bar, you'll love it as a garnish on top of this oaty, peanutty bar.

½ cup (1 stick) unsalted butter

⅓ cup peanut butter

1 cup brown sugar

1 egg

½ tsp. vanilla extract

1 cup all-purpose flour

1 cup rolled oats

½ tsp. baking soda

½ tsp. kosher salt

1 recipe Chocolate Ganache, room temperature (see Chapter 3)

1-2 Butterfinger candy bars, frozen

> **Makes about 12 to 15 bars**
>
> **Prep Time:** 30 minutes
>
> **Cook Time:** 20 minutes, plus 1 hour cooling time

1. Preheat the oven to 350°F. Coat a 9×13 pan with nonstick cooking spray.

2. In a large bowl, beat together butter, peanut butter, and brown sugar until smooth and creamy. Add egg and vanilla.

3. In a separate bowl, stir together flour, oats, baking soda, and salt, then add to the batter and mix thoroughly.

4. Press into prepared pan and bake 15 to 20 minutes until golden brown and firm to the touch. Cool completely.

5. Crush the frozen candy bars in their wrappers with a rolling pin. Ice the top of the bars with ganache and sprinkle with crushed candy bars. Chill at least one hour before cutting into bars.

Helpful Hints

Candy shatters into cleaner bits when frozen than when room temperature. Although the wrappers are kept on, you can avoid a big mess by placing them inside one or two plastic bags before crushing.

Chocolate-Covered Pretzel Bars

The snack phenomenon of chocolate-covered pretzels has taken the country by storm. Treat your food-fad family to this easy sweet and salty layered bar.

2 cups pretzels, crushed

½ cup (1 stick) unsalted butter, melted

2 cups chocolate chips

½ cup chopped peanuts

1 (14-oz.) can sweetened condensed milk

Makes about 12 to 15 bars

Prep Time: 10 minutes

Cook Time: 30 minutes, plus 30 minutes cooling time

1. Preheat the oven to 350°F. Coat a 9×13 pan with nonstick cooking spray.

2. Combine crushed pretzels and melted butter and press into prepared pan. Sprinkle with chocolate chips and peanuts, then drizzle condensed milk evenly over all.

3. Bake 25 to 30 minutes until golden brown. Cool completely, then refrigerate at least 30 minutes before cutting into bars.

Helpful Hints

Chunkier pretzels work better in this recipe than pulverized ones. To crush them, place pretzels into one or two plastic zipper bags, then pound gently with a rolling pin.

Coconut Dream Bars

This bar consists of a buttery, crisp pastry crust with a not-too-sweet nutty topping. It is super easy and super good.

1 cup (2 sticks) unsalted butter

2 cups brown sugar, divided

1¾ cups all-purpose flour, divided

½ tsp. baking powder

¼ tsp. kosher salt

2 eggs

1 tsp. vanilla

1 cup shredded coconut

1 cup pecans

Makes about 12 to 15 bars

Prep Time: 30 minutes

Cook Time: 40 minutes

1. Preheat the oven to 350°F. Coat a 9×13 pan with nonstick cooking spray.

2. Combine one cup melted butter, ¾ cup brown sugar, and 1½ cups all-purpose flour. Mix well and press into prepared pan.

3. Bake 10 minutes.

4. Combine remaining brown sugar, flour, baking powder, salt, eggs, and vanilla and beat until smooth. Fold in coconut and pecans; spread over crust.

5. Bake another 20 to 30 minutes until golden brown. Cool completely before cutting into bars.

Helpful Hints

Coconut comes in many forms. It can be sweetened or unsweetened, shredded large, small, or desiccated (small granules). Any of these will work well in this recipe because the coconut is folded into a batter. Sweetened coconut will add more sugar; unsweetened will tone it down. When decorating the tops of desserts with coconut, however, sweetened is preferred.

Date Bars

These sweet, chewy bars are sturdy and long lasting. They make perfect care packages to send to your favorite college student.

1 egg

1 cup sugar

½ tsp. kosher salt

½ cup milk

1 TB. vanilla

2 tsp. baking powder

1 cup all-purpose flour

1½ cups dates, pitted and chopped

1 cup pecans

2 cups powdered sugar, sifted

Makes about 12 to 15 bars
Prep Time: 30 minutes
Cook Time: 30 minutes

1. Preheat the oven to 350°F. Coat a 9×13 pan with nonstick cooking spray.

2. In a large bowl, stir together egg and sugar. Add salt, milk, and vanilla; stir to combine.

3. Sift together baking powder and flour and mix well. Fold in dates and pecans.

4. Pour batter into prepared pan and bake until golden brown, 20 to 30 minutes. Cool completely, cut into bars, and roll each bar in powdered sugar.

Tidbits

Dates have been an important food since pre-history and were the sweet treat of choice for ancient peoples. They are good sources of potassium, fiber, and B-complex vitamins.

Fluffernutter Bars

A Fluffernutter is a peanut butter and marshmallow fluff sandwich. Marshmallow fluff is a product available mainly on the East Coast. If you live in the west, you can use marshmallow creme or order it by mail (see Appendix B).

½ cup (1 stick) unsalted butter

½ cup peanut butter

1 cup brown sugar

1 egg

1¼ cups all-purpose flour

1½ tsp. baking powder

½ tsp. kosher salt

2 cups marshmallow fluff

2 cups roasted peanuts

Makes about 12 to 15 bars

Prep Time: 30 minutes

Cook Time: 25 minutes

1. Preheat the oven to 350°F. Coat a 9×13 pan with nonstick cooking spray.

2. In a large bowl, beat together butter, peanut butter, and brown sugar until smooth and creamy. Stir in egg, then add flour, baking powder, and salt.

3. Mix until just combined, then press into prepared baking dish. Bake for 10 to 15 minutes, until golden brown and firm to the touch.

4. Remove from oven and top with marshmallow and peanuts. Bake another 5 to 10 minutes until lightly browned. Cool completely before cutting into bars.

Key Lime Bars

The cheesecake-like consistency of this bar is the perfect platform for the tropically tart flavor of lime.

1 cup graham cracker crumbs

½ cup shredded coconut

3 TB. unsalted butter, melted

1 (8-oz.) pkg. cream cheese, softened

1 (14-oz.) can sweetened condensed milk

¼ cup key lime juice

Grated zest of 2 limes

Powdered sugar for dusting

> **Makes about 12 to 15 bars**
>
> **Prep Time:** 30 minutes
>
> **Cook Time:** 40 minutes, plus 2 hours cooling time

1. Preheat the oven to 350°F. Coat a 9×13 pan with nonstick cooking spray.

2. Combine graham cracker crumbs, coconut, and melted butter and mix until thoroughly moistened. Press into prepared pan and bake for 10 minutes until barely browned.

Tidbits

The key lime also is known as the Mexican lime. It is smaller than the standard lime, and it ripens yellow instead of green.

3. In a large bowl, beat cream cheese until smooth and lump-free. Add sweetened condensed milk, lime juice, and zest and mix well.

4. Spread evenly over crust and bake 20 to 30 minutes until set in the center. Cool completely, then chill at least two hours before cutting into bars. Dust with powdered sugar before serving.

Lemon Bars

These classic bars taste like mini lemon pies. The buttery crust and tart filling always sells out at bake sales.

1 cup (2 sticks) unsalted butter

2 cups all-purpose flour

½ cup powdered sugar

4 eggs

2 cups sugar

¼ cup lemon juice (about 3 medium lemons)

Grated zest of 2 lemons

Powdered sugar for dusting

> **Makes about 12 to 15 bars**
>
> **Prep Time:** 30 minutes
>
> **Cook Time:** 35 minutes, plus 1 hour cooling time

1. Preheat the oven to 325°F. Coat a 9×13 pan with nonstick cooking spray.

2. Combine flour and powdered sugar and cut in butter until it resembles a fine meal.

3. Press into prepared pan and bake for 10 minutes until lightly browned.

4. In a large bowl, whisk together eggs, sugar, lemon juice, and zest. Pour over browned crust.

5. Return to the oven for another 20 to 25 minutes until set and lightly browned. Cool completely, then chill at least one hour before cutting into bars. Dust with powdered sugar before serving.

Milk Chocolate Caramel Bars

This bar tastes like your favorite candy bar with an added cookie crust bonus. Be sure to chill it completely for the best-looking slices.

3 oz. (¾ stick) unsalted butter

1 cup brown sugar

1 egg

1¼ cups all-purpose flour

½ tsp. baking soda

½ tsp. kosher salt

1 cup caramel topping

1 recipe Seven-Minute Icing, milk chocolate variation (see Chapter 3)

1 recipe Chocolate Ganache, glaze variation (see Chapter 3)

> **Makes about 12 to 15 bars**
>
> **Prep Time:** 45 minutes
>
> **Cook Time:** 10 minutes, plus 2½ hours cooling time

1. Preheat the oven to 350°F. Coat a 9×13 pan with nonstick cooking spray.

2. In a large bowl, beat together butter and brown sugar until smooth and creamy. Stir in egg, then add flour, baking soda, and salt. Mix until just combined.

3. Press into prepared baking dish. Bake for 10 minutes until golden brown and firm to the touch.

4. Evenly distribute caramel over browned crust. Spread milk chocolate Seven-Minute Icing over bars, smoothly and evenly, and chill 30 minutes.

5. Finish with a topping of ganache glaze, spread evenly over all. Chill at least two hours before cutting into bars.

Seven-Layer Bars

These bars are super sweet and a little gooey. They are perfect for a late-night sweet tooth. They are also top sellers at bake sales.

¼ cup (½ stick) unsalted butter, melted

1 cup graham cracker crumbs

1 cup shredded coconut

1 cup chocolate chips

1 cup butterscotch chips

1 cup white chocolate chips

1 cup pecans

1 (15-oz.) can sweetened condensed milk

> **Makes about 12 to 15 bars**
>
> **Prep Time:** 10 minutes
>
> **Cook Time:** 30 minutes, plus 2 hours cooling time

1. Preheat the oven to 325°F. Coat a 9×13 pan with nonstick cooking spray.

2. In the prepared pan, spread even layers of butter, graham cracker crumbs, coconut, chocolate chips, butterscotch chips, white chocolate chips, and pecans.

3. Drizzle sweetened condensed milk evenly over all, and bake 25 to 30 minutes until golden brown.

4. Cool completely, then chill at least two hours before cutting.

Spiderweb Bars

These bars are really just fancy-pants brownies. The web design is an easy pastry trick that always wows the crowd.

½ cup (1 stick) unsalted butter

½ cup chocolate chips

¾ cup sugar

2 eggs

½ tsp. vanilla extract

½ tsp. baking soda

½ tsp. kosher salt

½ cup all-purpose flour

1 cup white chocolate chips

1 recipe Chocolate Ganache, glaze variation (see Chapter 3)

> **Makes about 12 to 15 bars**
>
> **Prep Time:** 30 minutes
>
> **Cook Time:** 25 minutes, plus 2 hours cooling time

1. Preheat the oven to 325°F. Coat a 9×13 pan with nonstick cooking spray.

2. Melt butter and chocolate together over low heat, stirring until completely melted. Remove from heat and beat in sugar, eggs, and vanilla.

3. Sift together baking soda, salt, and flour and beat into batter. Transfer to prepared baking pan, spread smoothly, and bake 20 to 25 minutes until firm. Cool completely.

4. Using a glass or ceramic dish, melt white chocolate chips in the microwave, stirring every 5 to 10 seconds until smooth and lump-free. Set aside.

5. Pour warm ganache glaze over baked brownies and spread smoothly. Cover the ganache with thin, straight lines of drizzled warm white chocolate, covering the entire surface in one direction. Quickly use a toothpick to draw perpendicular lines through the white chocolate every one inch. Next, draw the toothpick in the opposite direction between the first lines. Chill at least two hours before cutting into bars.

Heads Up

White chocolate burns easily and tends to clump when overheated. Watch it carefully, and stir frequently.

Chapter 7

Brownies

In This Chapter

- ◆ Dark, milk, and white chocolate brownies
- ◆ Classic flavor combinations
- ◆ Smooth and silky, chewy and chunky

Brownies are quite possibly the most popular bakery item on Earth. Dark and chocolaty, rich and decadent, but still modest and commonplace, brownies satisfy like no cookie or cake possibly can. No matter how you like your brownies, there should be at least one recipe in this chapter that satisfies your desire.

Brownie Background

The first brownie is generally thought to have been a mistake—a chocolate cake gone bad. Many apocryphal tales of this event are told, dating back to the 1890s. Many of these tales reveal cookies or cakes flavored not with chocolate but with molasses, nuts, and spices. The brownie as we know it today wasn't popular until the 1920s.

With any popular recipe, there are camps of preference. Cakey, gooey, fudgy, and chewy all have their cheerleaders, and there are a plethora of recipes for each kind.

Fudgy brownies seem to be the overall favorite incarnation. To achieve a fudgy brownie, the flour is minimized, the leavening is omitted, and butter is added in melted form rather than being creamed. If you prefer a cakelike brownie, add more flour, a little baking powder, and cream the butter and sugar together. The chocolate plays a role, too. Cocoa powder is a drier form and generally creates a drier finished product. Bittersweet, semisweet, and unsweetened chocolates taste different but also provide different effects based on their fat content.

If you are intrigued by these variants, there is no better recipe to experiment with than the brownie. Its ingredients are few, and the outcome—whether successful or not—is always welcome.

Blondies

Blondies are blonde brownies. They are sometimes made with chocolate chips, but more common is this butterscotch version. Chewy in the center and crisp on the edges, they are an American favorite.

2¾ cups all-purpose flour

1 tsp. baking soda

½ tsp. kosher salt

6 oz. (1½ sticks) butter

1 cup sugar

1 cup brown sugar

1 TB. vanilla extract

2 eggs

2 cups butterscotch chips

> **Makes 12 to 15 bars**
>
> **Prep Time:** 30 minutes
>
> **Cook Time:** 30 minutes

1. Preheat the oven to 325°F. Coat two 9×13 pans with nonstick cooking spray.

2. Beat butter and sugars together until smooth and creamy. Add vanilla and eggs one by one.

3. Sift together flour, baking soda, and salt and slowly add. Mix well to fully incorporate; fold in chips.

4. Transfer batter to prepared pan and bake 20 to 25 minutes until golden brown on the edges. Cool completely before cutting.

 **Tidbits**

Butterscotch was an enormously popular flavor in the late 1800s. It wasn't until the 1920s that chocolate became the world's favorite sweet.

Chocolate Fudge Brownies

This is the classic brownie recipe with a twist. They are baked thin and sandwiched with rich bittersweet ganache.

1 cup (2 sticks) unsalted butter

1 cup chocolate chips

1½ cups sugar

4 eggs

1 tsp. vanilla extract

1 tsp. baking soda

1 tsp. kosher salt

1 cup all-purpose flour

1 recipe Chocolate Ganache, room temperature (see Chapter 3)

Makes about 12 to 15 brownies

Prep Time: 30 minutes

Cook Time: 25 minutes, plus 1 hour cooling time

1. Preheat the oven to 325°F. Coat two 9×13 pans with nonstick cooking spray.

2. Melt butter and chocolate together over low heat, stirring until completely melted. Remove from heat and beat in sugar, eggs, and vanilla.

3. Sift together baking soda, salt, and flour and beat into batter.

4. Divide evenly between both prepared pans, spread smoothly, and bake 20 to 25 minutes until firm. Cool completely.

5. Spread ganache evenly over one pan of brownies. Invert second pan of brownies on top of ganache and press to sandwich ganache between brownies. Chill at least one hour before slicing into squares.

Variations

 ◆ **Nuts to You:** These brownies will hold up to 1½ cups of chopped nuts (if that's your thing). Classic additions include pecans or walnuts, but why not be a bit daring and try Brazil nuts, cashews, or hazelnuts.

Chocolate Mint Brownies

Chocolate and mint were made to go together. This recipe is reminiscent of an after-dinner mint.

1 cup (2 sticks) butter, divided

1 cup sugar

2 cups chocolate syrup

4 eggs

1 tsp. vanilla extract

$\frac{1}{2}$ tsp. kosher salt

1 cup all-purpose flour

$2\frac{1}{2}$ cups powdered sugar

$\frac{1}{4}$ cup *crème de menthe*

1-2 drops green food color (optional)

1 recipe Chocolate Ganache, glaze variation (see Chapter 3)

> **Makes about 12 to 15 brownies**
>
> **Prep Time:** 45 minutes
>
> **Cook Time:** 30 minutes

1. Preheat the oven to 325°F. Coat a 9×13 pan with nonstick cooking spray.

2. Beat together $\frac{1}{2}$ cup butter and sugar until smooth and creamy. Add eggs one by one, then vanilla and salt.

3. Sift flour and stir until fully incorporated.

4. Spread into prepared pan and bake 25 to 30 minutes until firm. Cool.

5. Melt remaining butter in a large saucepan over medium heat. Remove from heat; stir in powdered sugar, crème de menthe, and food color if desired.

6. Spread evenly over baked brownies and chill for at least 30 minutes.

7. Spread ganache glaze over mint frosting and chill again for at least 30 minutes before cutting into squares.

Sweet Talk

Crème de menthe is a mint-flavored liqueur that is available in clear or green versions. It was traditionally made from Corsican mint, a Mediterranean native that is similar in flavor to peppermint.

Marble Brownies

This classic recipe uses cream cheese, which creates a universally beloved cheesecake-like element.

¾ cup (1½ sticks) unsalted butter

2 cups sugar, divided

3 tsp. vanilla, divided

4 eggs, divided

¾ cup all-purpose flour

½ cup cocoa powder

1 tsp. baking powder

½ tsp. kosher salt

1 (8-oz.) pkg. cream cheese

1 cup chocolate chips

Makes about 12 to 15 brownies

Prep Time: 35 minutes

Cook Time: 30 minutes

1. Preheat the oven to 350°F. Coat a 9×13 pan with nonstick cooking spray.

2. Beat together butter and 1½ cups sugar until smooth and creamy. Add 1½ teaspoons vanilla, then three eggs one by one.

3. Sift together flour, cocoa powder, and salt and stir into batter. Pour into prepared pan and set aside.

4. Beat cream cheese until smooth and lump-free. Add remaining sugar, remaining vanilla, and remaining egg, incorporating fully.

5. Distribute dollops evenly across the top of the brownies, then swirl with the tip of the knife. Bake 25 to 30 minutes until firm. Cool 20 minutes before cutting into squares.

Variations

◆ **Pumpkin Marble:** A favorite in the fall, add one cup pumpkin puree and one teaspoon pumpkin pie spice to the cream cheese swirl.

◆ **Mocha Marble:** For coffee lovers, add two tablespoons instant espresso powder to the cream cheese swirl.

Mexican Chocolate Brownies

Mexican chocolate, used traditionally for exquisite hot cocoa, is loaded with cinnamon. The flavor combination is deliciously exotic.

¾ cup unsalted butter

1½ cups sugar

1½ tsp. vanilla

3 eggs

½ cup cocoa powder

¾ cup all-purpose flour

½ tsp. baking powder

1 tsp. kosher salt

1 TB. cinnamon, divided

½ cup brown sugar

1 cup toasted pecans, chopped

> **Makes about 12 to 16 brownies**
>
> **Prep Time:** 20 minutes
> **Cook Time:** 30 minutes

1. Preheat the oven to 350°F. Coat a 9×13 pan with nonstick cooking spray.

2. Beat together butter and sugar until smooth and creamy. Add vanilla, then add eggs one by one.

3. Sift together cocoa, flour, baking powder, salt, and one tablespoon of cinnamon and stir into batter. Pour into prepared pan and set aside.

4. Combine remaining cinnamon, brown sugar, and pecans and sprinkle evenly over batter. Bake 20 to 30 minutes until firm. Cool completely before cutting.

Tidbits

Mexican chocolate is made by coarsely grinding cocoa beans with thick crystals of sugar and crushed cinnamon sticks. It is sold in discs and is meant to be melted or dissolved in hot water, milk, or molé (sauce). Eaten raw, its texture is strangely coarse—but the flavor is uniquely wonderful.

Orange-Chocolate Brownies

Fragrant orange zest, tangy orange juice, and deep dark chocolate is a classic, delicious combination.

¼ cup (½ stick) unsalted butter

½ cup chocolate chips

Grated zest of 2 oranges

¾ cup sugar

2 eggs

¼ orange juice concentrate

¾ cup all-purpose flour

¼ tsp. baking soda

¼ tsp. kosher salt

1 recipe Chocolate Ganache, glaze variation (see Chapter 3)

¼ cup *Grand Marnier*

> **Makes about 12 to 16 brownies**
>
> **Prep Time:** 30 minutes
>
> **Cook Time:** 30 minutes, plus 1 hour cooling time

1. Preheat the oven to 350°F. Coat a 9×13 pan with nonstick cooking spray.

2. Melt butter, chocolate, and orange zest together in a large saucepan over medium heat, stirring. Remove from heat; add sugar, eggs, and orange juice and beat until smooth.

3. Sift together flour, baking soda, and salt and stir into batter. Transfer batter to prepared pan and spread smoothly.

4. Bake 25 to 30 minutes until firm to the touch. Cool completely.

5. Stir together ganache glaze and Grand Marnier and spread evenly on top of cooled brownies. Chill at least one hour before cutting.

Sweet Talk

Grand Marnier is an orange liqueur made from *cognac* and orange essence. There are several other similarly flavored liqueurs, including Cointreau and Triple Sec.

Raspberry Brownies

Here is another classic flavor combination. The tartness of the berries cuts through the rich chocolate in dignified balance.

1 cup (2 sticks) unsalted butter

1½ cups chocolate chips

2 cups sugar

4 eggs

2 tsp. vanilla

1¼ cups all-purpose flour

1 tsp. baking powder

¼ tsp. kosher salt

1 pint fresh raspberries

1 recipe Chocolate Ganache, glaze variation (see Chapter 3)

1 cup raspberry jam

Makes about 12 to 16 brownies

Prep Time: 30 minutes

Cook Time: 30 minutes, plus 1 hour cooling time

1. Preheat the oven to 350°F. Coat a 9×13 pan with nonstick cooking spray.

2. Melt butter and chocolate together in a large saucepan over medium heat, stirring. Remove from heat; add sugar, eggs, and vanilla and beat until smooth.

3. Sift together flour, baking powder, and salt and stir into batter. Fold in berries.

4. Transfer to prepared pan and spread smoothly. Bake 25 to 30 minutes until firm to the touch. Cool completely.

5. Stir together Chocolate Ganache glaze and raspberry jam, and spread evenly on top of cooled brownies. Chill at least one hour before cutting.

Variations

◆ **Tutti Frutti:** The tart raspberry can be substituted with any number of fruits that have similar characteristics. Try cranberries, apricots, pineapple, or rhubarb.

Rocky Road Brownies

This chunky combination of almonds, marshmallows, and chocolate need not be limited to the freezer. These brownies make a perfect pick-me-up treat when the road gets bumpy.

¾ cup (1½ sticks) unsalted butter

1 square unsweetened chocolate

1½ cups sugar, divided

2 eggs, divided

1 tsp. vanilla

1 cup plus 2 TB. all-purpose flour

1 tsp. baking powder

¼ tsp. kosher salt

½ cup chopped almonds

1 (8-oz.) pkg. cream cheese

1 cup chocolate chips

2 cups mini marshmallows

Makes about 12 to 16 brownies

Prep Time: 30 minutes

Cook Time: 30 minutes

1. Preheat the oven to 350°F. Coat a 9×13 pan with nonstick cooking spray.

2. Melt ½ cup butter and chocolate together in a large saucepan over medium heat, stirring. Remove from heat; add one cup sugar, one egg, and vanilla and beat until smooth.

3. Sift together flour, baking powder, and salt and stir into batter. Transfer to prepared pan and spread smoothly. Set aside.

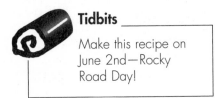

Tidbits

Make this recipe on June 2nd—Rocky Road Day!

4. In a separate bowl, beat together cream cheese and remaining butter until smooth. Beat in remaining sugar and egg. Fold in chocolate chips and marshmallows and spread evenly over batter.

5. Bake 25 to 30 minutes until firm to the touch. Cool completely.

White Chocolate Macadamia Brownies

It was cookies that made this flavor duo famous, but they work together equally well in brownie form. The rich macadamia nut seems to have been created for this very snack.

6 TB. (¾ stick) unsalted butter

1½ cups white chocolate chips

2 eggs

½ cup sugar

1 TB. vanilla extract

1 cup all-purpose flour

¼ tsp. kosher salt

1½ cups toasted macadamia nuts, chopped

> **Makes about 12 to 16 brownies**
>
> **Prep Time:** 30 minutes
>
> **Cook Time:** 30 minutes

1. Preheat the oven to 350°F. Coat a 9×13 pan with nonstick cooking spray.

2. Melt butter in a medium saucepan over medium heat. Remove from heat, add white chocolate chips, and stir until melted. Set aside.

3. With an electric mixer or hand whisk, whip eggs and sugar together until pale and fluffy (about five minutes). Add white chocolate, vanilla, flour, and salt. Fold in nuts and transfer to prepared pan.

4. Bake for 25 to 30 minutes until firm to the touch. Cool completely.

Variations

- White chocolate also benefits from tart or acidic fruit. Try folding in dried cranberries, tart cherries, or fresh raspberries.

Tidbits

White chocolate is not technically considered chocolate because it contains only cocoa butter and not cocoa bean solids.

Chapter 8

Squares

In This Chapter

- ◆ Creamy, rich, and fruity squares
- ◆ Chunky, nutty, and crunchy squares
- ◆ Candy, soda, and popcorn squares

For years, the term *square* was a derogatory comment meant to make you feel lame, bogus, and uncool. Fortunately for this chapter, that is no longer the case. Square as a put-down has gone the way of bell-bottoms and fringed leather vests.

These squares are the epitome of the snack cake. Made quickly and easily in rectangular baking dishes, these cakes are cut into squares and nibbled on the go. All you need is a sturdy napkin and a sweet tooth.

Square One

Of course, to call anything a square you must cut it into that shape. But the size of your square can be determined by the occasion. For snacking, two-inch squares are appropriate. Richer recipes topped with chocolate ganache or baked with cream cheese can be cut even smaller.

For buffet presentations or tea tray arrangements, the key to good-looking squares is uniformity. To cut all of your squares the same size, start by cutting the entire pan in half. Then, divide each section in half until you have strips of cake in the width you want. Then, turn the pan and repeat in the opposite direction.

For squares with gooey toppings, dip your knife in hot water and wipe it clean after each cut. This will help keep your cuts clean and smooth and keep the top of the cake free of crumbs.

Getting a Round

All of these recipes bake nicely in any shaped pan, and for use as a dessert course, a wedge of cake is sometimes a more pleasing presentation—topped with a dollop of cream, a spoonful of fresh fruit, or a sprinkling of nuts. Serving cakes in this way transforms them from after school to after dinner in the blink of an eye.

If you are inclined to go round, use a 9- to 10-inch round cake pan, and prepare it in the same manner as you would any other pan you might use for baking: with a generous coating of nonstick cooking spray.

Apricot Upside-Down Squares

Sweet, juicy apricots are the perfect match for this delicate, buttery cake. Buy them at the height of the season, usually late spring or early summer, for the best results.

½ cup brown sugar, packed

6-8 fresh apricots, sliced in wedges

½ cup (1 stick) unsalted butter

1 cup sugar

1 egg

½ tsp. vanilla extract

1¾ cups all-purpose flour

1 tsp. baking soda

½ tsp. kosher salt

1 cup evaporated milk

> **Makes 12 to 16 squares**
>
> **Prep Time:** 20 minutes
>
> **Cook Time:** 40 minutes

1. Preheat the oven to 350°F. Coat a 9×13 pan with nonstick cooking spray. Sprinkle brown sugar evenly across the bottom of the pan, and top with neatly arranged apricot wedges. Set aside.

2. Beat butter and sugar until smooth and creamy. Add egg and vanilla.

3. In a separate bowl, sift together flour, baking soda, and salt and add alternately with milk. Pour batter over apricots.

4. Bake 25 to 30 minutes until firm and a pick inserted in the center comes out clean. Cool 10 minutes, then invert and cut into squares.

Variations

◆ **Apricot Almond Upside-Down Squares:** Arrange one cup of sliced almonds with the apricots, and add ¼ cup of amaretto to the batter.

Helpful Hints

Apricots do not need to be peeled. Their skin is thin and tender and is not at all noticeable.

Butterscotch Chocolate Nut Bars

Like a candy bar, these squares combine caramelicious butterscotch with peanuts and chocolate.

1¼ cups unsalted butter

2 cups brown sugar

⅓ cup corn syrup

8 cups rolled oats

2 tsp. vanilla extract

1½ cups peanut butter, divided

1 cup chocolate chips

1 cup butterscotch chips

1 cup peanuts

**Makes about
24 squares**

Prep Time: 15 minutes

Cook Time: 20 minutes, plus 1 hour cooling

1. Preheat the oven to 350°F. Coat a 9×13 pan with nonstick cooking spray.

2. In a large saucepan, combine butter, brown sugar, corn syrup, oats, vanilla, and ¾ cup peanut butter. Stir together over medium heat until melted and well blended. Transfer to prepared pan.

3. Bake 15 to 20 minutes until firm. Cool completely.

4. In a large saucepan over low heat, stir together chocolate chips, butterscotch chips, and remaining peanut butter until melted and smooth. Spread over the top of baked bars, and top with chopped peanuts.

5. Chill at least one hour before cutting into squares.

Chocolate Chip Squares

Chocolate chips suspended in chocolate batter is a chocolate lover's dream. Top it off with chocolate ganache and you're in hog heaven!

¾ cup (1½ sticks) unsalted butter

2 cups sugar

2 eggs

2 tsp. vanilla extract

2 cups all-purpose flour

¾ cup cocoa powder

1 tsp. baking soda

½ tsp. kosher salt

2 cups chocolate chips

1 recipe Chocolate Ganache, glaze variation (see Chapter 3)

> **Makes about 24 squares**
>
> **Prep Time:** 20 minutes
>
> **Cook Time:** 25 minutes, plus 1 hour cooling time

1. Preheat the oven to 350°F. Coat a 9×13 pan with nonstick cooking spray.

2. Beat together butter and sugar until smooth and creamy. Add eggs one by one, then add vanilla.

3. Sift together flour, cocoa, baking soda, and salt and stir into batter. Fold in chocolate chips.

4. Transfer dough to prepared pan and bake 20 to 25 minutes until golden brown and firm. Cool completely.

5. Spread ganache glaze smoothly over the top. Chill at least one hour before cutting into squares.

Variations

◆ **Chocolate Heaven:** For a change of pace, add a variety of chocolate chips. Choose dark, milk, or white chocolate chips—or mix them together to equal two cups.

Crème de Menthe Squares

These squares are sweet and decadent with a crunchy bottom and a rich, chocolaty top. Serve in small squares.

½ cup unsalted butter

¼ cup cocoa powder

3½ cups powdered sugar, divided

2 cups graham cracker crumbs

¼ cup crème de menthe

1 recipe Chocolate Ganache, glaze variation (see Chapter 3)

> **Makes about 24 squares**
>
> **Prep Time:** 30 minutes, plus 2 hours cooling time

1. Coat a 9×13 pan with nonstick cooking spray.

2. In a large saucepan, melt ¼ cup butter over low heat. Remove from heat; beat in cocoa powder, ¼ cup powdered sugar, and graham cracker crumbs.

3. Press into prepared pan and chill until firm (about 30 minutes).

4. Melt remaining butter with crème de menthe over low heat. Remove from heat; beat in remaining powdered sugar until smooth and creamy.

5. Spread smoothly across bottom layer, then chill 30 minutes.

6. Cover with ganache glaze and chill at least one hour before cutting into squares.

Variations

◆ **Liqueurs:** There are several liqueurs that taste just as good with chocolate as mint does. Omit the crème de menthe and try Cointreau (orange), Chartreuse (herb), Frangelico (hazelnut), amaretto (almond), Kahlúa (coffee), Sambuca (anise), Chambord (raspberry), or crème de cassis (black currant).

Espresso Squares

This simple cake is loaded with coffee flavor. It's a fantastic choice for breakfast, brunch, or tea time. And it just may help your student through late-night study sessions.

1 cup (2 sticks) unsalted butter

1½ cups sugar

4 large eggs

3 cups all-purpose flour

2 tsp. baking powder

½ tsp. kosher salt

1 cup milk

3 TB. coffee extract or instant espresso powder

⅓ cup brown sugar

⅓ cup instant coffee crystals

Makes about 24 squares

Prep Time: 20 minutes

Cook Time: 40 minutes

1. Preheat oven to 350°F. Coat a 9×13 pan with nonstick cooking spray.

2. Beat butter and sugar together until smooth and creamy. Add eggs one at a time.

3. Combine flour, baking powder, and salt; set aside.

4. Stir together milk and coffee extract (or espresso powder) and add to creamed mixture alternately with flour mixture. Transfer batter to pan.

5. Combine brown sugar and coffee crystals and sprinkle evenly on top of batter.

6. Bake 30 to 40 minutes until firm and a pick inserted in the center comes out clean. Cool completely.

Variations

◆ This cake would be lovely with a thin coating of Chocolate Ganache, a light dollop of Whipped Cream, or both! (See Chapter 3.)

Gingerbread

Christmas doesn't come to our house unless the smell of this cake is wafting through the air. The lemon icing is the perfect accompaniment, setting off the rich, spicy cake with a pleasant tartness.

6 oz. (1½ sticks) butter

¼ cup brown sugar

1 egg

1 cup molasses

1 cup hot water

2⅓ cups all-purpose flour

1½ tsp. baking soda

½ tsp. kosher salt

1 tsp. ground ginger

1 tsp. cinnamon

1 tsp. nutmeg

½ tsp. cloves

2 (1-lb.) boxes powdered sugar, sifted

Grated zest of one lemon

¼ cup lemon juice

1 TB. milk

Makes about 10 to 12 squares

Prep Time: 20 minutes

Cook Time: 40 minutes

Finishing Time: 20 minutes

1. Preheat the oven to 350°F. Coat a 9×13 pan with nonstick cooking spray.

2. Beat together four ounces (one stick) butter and sugar until smooth and creamy. Add egg and mix well.

3. Combine water and molasses and set aside.

4. Sift together flour, baking soda, salt, ginger, cinnamon, nutmeg, and cloves and add alternately with the molasses. Blend until smooth.

5. Pour into prepared pan and bake 30 to 40 minutes until a pick inserted in the center comes out clean. Cool completely.

6. Cream together remaining butter and half the powdered sugar until smooth and lump-free. Slowly add lemon zest, juice, and milk and blend until smooth. Add remaining sugar and beat until fluffy. Adjust consistency with more sugar or milk as needed.

7. Spread frosting evenly onto gingerbread. To serve, slice into squares.

 Heads Up

Don't get lazy. The most important aspect of this recipe is sifting the powdered sugar for the frosting. If you don't, the outcome will be lumpy and most unattractive.

Red, White, and Blueberry Squares

These squares have a crisp and nutty oat base topped with cheesecake and studded with sweet, ripe berries.

1 cup rolled oats

¾ cup all-purpose flour

⅓ cup brown sugar

¼ cup walnuts, chopped

¼ tsp. baking soda

¼ tsp. kosher salt

6 TB. (¼ stick) unsalted butter, melted

2 (8-oz.) pkgs. cream cheese, softened

¾ cup sugar

2 TB. all-purpose flour

2 eggs

1 tsp. vanilla extract

1 pint fresh raspberries

1 pint fresh blueberries

> **Makes about 24 squares**
>
> **Prep Time:** 30 minutes
>
> **Cook Time:** 30 minutes, plus 2 hours cooling time

1. Preheat the oven to 350°F. Coat a 9×13 pan with nonstick cooking spray.

2. In a large bowl, mix together oats, flour, brown sugar, walnuts, baking soda, and salt. Add melted butter and stir to moisten. Press into prepared pan and bake 10 minutes until lightly browned.

3. Beat together cream cheese and sugar until smooth and creamy. Mix in eggs one by one and then vanilla. Spread on top of crust.

4. Distribute berries evenly across the surface and press into cheesecake gently.

5. Bake 15 to 20 minutes until cheese is set and just begins to brown. Cool completely, then chill at least two hours before cutting and serving.

Variations

◆ **Peachy Keen:** These squares work well with lots of fruits, including peaches, cherries, and plums.

Root Beer Float Cake

If you're a fan of root beer, you'll love this cake. Complete the effect by serving it with a scoop of vanilla ice cream.

1 cup (2 sticks) unsalted butter

1½ cups brown sugar

2 tsp. root beer extract

4 eggs

2½ cups all-purpose flour

2½ tsp. baking powder

1 tsp. kosher salt

1 (12-oz.) can root beer

1 recipe White Frosting (see Chapter 3) plus 1 TB. root beer extract

> **Makes about 24 squares**
>
> **Prep Time:** 20 minutes
>
> **Cook Time:** 35 minutes, plus 30 minutes cooling time

1. Preheat the oven to 350°F. Coat a 9×13 pan with nonstick cooking spray.

2. Beat together butter, sugar, and extract until smooth and creamy, then add eggs one by one.

3. Sift together flour, baking powder, and salt and add alternately with one cup root beer.

4. Transfer to prepared pan and bake until firm to the touch, about 30 to 35 minutes. Cool completely.

5. Stir remaining root beer into White Frosting and spread over top of cake. Chill 30 minutes before cutting into squares.

 Helpful Hints

The key to this recipe is the root beer extract, which can be found at specialty markets or ordered online (see Appendix B).

S'mores Cake

This snack cake offers all the fun of camping without having to build a fire.

½ cup (1 stick) unsalted butter

¾ cup sugar

2 eggs

1 tsp. vanilla extract

2 cups graham cracker crumbs

½ cup all-purpose flour

2½ tsp. baking powder

¾ cup milk

½ cup mini marshmallows

½ cup chocolate chips

Serves 8 to 10
Prep Time: 20 minutes
Cook Time: 30 minutes

1. Preheat the oven to 350°F. Coat a 9×13 pan with nonstick cooking spray.

2. Beat butter and sugar together until smooth and creamy. Add eggs one at a time, then add vanilla.

3. Stir together graham cracker crumbs, flour, and baking powder and add alternately with milk. Fold in marshmallows and chocolate chips.

4. Transfer batter to prepared pan and bake 25 to 30 minutes or until a pick inserted in the center comes out clean. Cool completely.

Variations

◆ **Marshmallow Mania:** Try frosting this cake with a generous helping of marshmallow creme and browning it under the broiler for a minute or two. The scouts will come knocking.

Part 4

Sweet Doughs

While not technically snack "cakes," the recipes in these chapters represent the best of sweet snacking. Doughnuts, cream puffs, and sweet rolls have all appeared in cellophane wrappers, and all hold a special place in our collective snacking hearts.

In this section, we discuss the intricacies of working with yeast—including kneading, fermentation, forming, baking, and frying. Chapter 10 is devoted to cream puffs, made from one classic dough called *pâte à choux*, which is the basis for sweet treats around the world. These recipes will not only round out your recipe files but will also instruct you in some basic skills that are useful in other culinary genres.

Chapter 9

Doughnuts

In This Chapter

- ◆ Cake and yeast doughnuts
- ◆ Circles, holes, and bars
- ◆ Plain, iced, and glazed

Every country that has dough has fried dough. Such delicacies likely originated from bakers looking for something to do with scrap pieces of dough. Some of them were dropped into soup, becoming dumplings. Some were baked into breadsticks or cookies. Some were incorporated into other larger recipes of dough. But the lucky ones were fried and doused with sugar.

In the world of doughnuts, there are two styles: yeast and cake. They are differentiated by the dough and the leavening used to raise them.

Yeast Doughnuts

Yeast doughnuts are made like bread dough. Yeast is combined with warm liquid, sugar, and flavorings. Flour is kneaded in for about 10 minutes until the dough is smooth and elastic, then it rises until it doubles in volume.

Yeast is a one-celled microorganism that feeds off sugar in the presence of a liquid at room temperature. The liquid can be any number of things, including water, milk, or even juice. It should be warm to the touch but not so hot that you can't dip your finger in it. If it's too hot for you, it will be too hot for the yeast. If you're the type who needs precision, it should be around 100°F—just above body temperature. The liquid can be heated on the stove or in the microwave. If it gets too hot, let it cool before adding so you do not kill the yeast. Hot tap water is a perfectly acceptable option.

The sugar can take several forms, including white, brown, or even honey. When yeast feeds on sugar, it creates carbon dioxide gas as a by product. This gas accumulates in the dough—which, if properly kneaded, expands to at least double its volume.

Kneading dough can be done in a variety of ways. Rolling, twisting, slapping, and folding all do the trick. The key is to keep agitating the dough while you move it around the counter. You will notice that as the kneading progresses, the dough will become increasingly smooth. While kneading, dough becomes elastic due to the presence of gluten, a protein that forms when wheat flour is manipulated with water. Without gluten, the dough will not rise and the structure of the finished product will be chewy and dense.

Cake Doughnuts

Cake doughnuts are mixed like—you guessed it—cake. Generally, the recipe begins with creaming butter and sugar together, adding eggs, and then adding the dry and wet ingredients. It is the same technique, known as the creaming method, used in cakes, muffins, and cookies.

It is important to avoid overworking this dough at any time during the process. Overcreaming the butter and sugar will make the dough runny. If you are creaming by hand, let the butter soften and mix it only until the lumps are gone. If you have an electric mixer, it's better to use cold butter. The excess friction from the machine can nearly liquefy softened butter, which will make the finished batter runny and hard to form.

Overworking cake dough once the flour is added can make the finished product tough. Gluten is not needed to provide structure for the leavening when no yeast is present, so it is not necessary to knead the cake dough.

Forming Dough

Once the dough is made, it must be rolled out and cut. Do this on a smooth, lightly floured surface. Working with manageable portions of dough, pat or roll it out with a rolling pin to a thickness of about one inch. Dip the doughnut cutters (or graduated circle cutters) in flour to ease the cutting process. After the dough is cut, scraps can be rerolled and recut—although the dough may need a short rest to relax the gluten and ease the rolling.

Cake dough must be chilled completely before it can be formed. The butter must have a chance to resolidify, and the flour must be given a chance to fully absorb all moisture. If the dough is not fully chilled, it will be sticky and nearly impossible to work with. Once cut, the scraps of cake dough can be rerolled and recut as well, although in this case, it may need to be refrigerated again before it can be easily rolled.

Deep Frying

If you do not have a deep-fat fryer, do not despair. Deep frying is easily accomplished on the stove. Use a heavy, high-sided pan. Cast iron is ideal because the heat is evenly distributed and held at an even temperature. The weight of cast iron makes it a safer choice because it is less likely to tip over. A heavy aluminum pan is another good choice. For safety's sake, be sure that pot handles are turned inward toward the wall.

Traditional frying was done with lard. As saturated fat fell out of favor, it was replaced by vegetable shortening. Now, we know that partially hydrogenated vegetable oil contains trans fat, which elevates cholesterol Therefore, the healthiest doughnuts (an oxymoron?) should be fried in canola oil, which is a monounsaturated oil.

Whenever you are deep-fat frying, it is important to regulate the oil's temperature. That does not necessarily mean you must continually check a thermometer. It does mean, however, that you must use your eyes and watch how fast the food is cooking. Browning should be gradual. If the food browns too quickly, turn down the flame and let the oil cool a bit.

If the oil is not hot enough, the food will soak it up, making your doughnuts greasy. Test the oil by dropping in a small bit of dough. If the oil is at 350° to 375°F, the dough will immediately begin to sizzle.

After they are fried, doughnuts should be properly drained before they are served. The easiest way to do this is to set them on a stack of paper towels for three to five minutes before glazing and serving.

Apple Fritters

Apples are the traditional flavor, but these crisp-fried fritters can be made with any fruit you like. Try pears, berries, peaches, and even bananas. Use your imagination!

4-6 cups canola oil

1 cup sifted all-purpose flour

$1/4$ cup sugar

1 tsp. kosher salt

$1^1/2$ tsp. baking powder

1 egg

2 large apples, peeled and grated

$1/2$ cup powdered sugar

Makes about 12 fritters
Prep Time: 30 minutes
Cook Time: 20 minutes

1. In a heavy, deep frying pan, heat canola oil to 350°F.

2. Sift together flour, sugar, salt, and baking powder into a large bowl.

3. In a separate bowl, whisk together egg and milk, then add to dry mixture and stir until just combined. Fold in apples.

4. Drop tablespoons of batter into hot oil and fry two to three minutes until evenly browned. Drain on paper towels and roll warm fritters in powdered sugar.

Helpful Hints

The fastest way to grate an apple is to peel it and grate down one side until you hit the core. Then, turn the apple and repeat on the remaining sides. Don't bother to quarter and core the apple first. It wastes time—and apple.

Beignets

In France, a beignet is fruit that is dipped in batter and fried (what we would call a fritter). But in the United States, beignet means New Orleans, the French Market, the Café du Monde, and chicory coffee. Don't you forget it!

¾ cup warm milk

1 (¼-oz.) pkg. granulated yeast

2 TB. honey

2 TB. melted butter

2-3 cups bread flour

4-6 cups canola oil

1 tsp. kosher salt

¼ cup powdered sugar

Makes about 12 beignets

Prep Time: 90 minutes

Cook Time: 20 minutes

1. Stir together milk, yeast, and honey and rest 10 minutes.

2. Add butter, one cup flour, and salt; stir together to form a smooth paste. Add remaining flour to form a firm dough.

3. Transfer to a floured work surface and knead vigorously for 8 to 10 minutes until smooth and elastic.

4. Return to bowl, dust with flour, cover with a warm, moist towel, and let rise until doubled in volume, about one hour.

5. In a heavy, deep frying pan, heat canola oil to 350°F.

6. Turn dough onto a floured surface, and with a rolling pin, roll to ¼-inch thick.

7. Cut into two-inch squares and fry in hot oil, one to two minutes on each side until evenly browned. Drain on paper towels.

8. Dust with powdered sugar before serving.

Ambrosia Cake

Chocolate
Peppermint Stick
Cupcakes

Chocolate Turtle
Cake

Coconut Cupcakes

Peanut Butter Cupcakes

Strawberry Shortcake Cupcakes

Pumpkin
Cream Cheese
Coffee Cake

S'mores Cake

Tropical Crumb Cake

Apricot Upside-Down Squares

Cherry Upside-Down Cake

Chocolate
Fudge
Brownies

Christmas
Fruitcake

Cream-Filled
Swan

Classic
Cream-Filled
Chocolate
Cupcakes

Doughnuts

Cream-Filled
Chocolate Roll

Jelly Roll

Mini
Blueberry Pie

Coffee Cream Puffs

Profiteroles

Marshmallow-Filled
Chocolate Sandwich

Red, White, and Blueberry Squares

Spiderweb Bars

Strawberry
Toaster Tarts

Coconut
Cream-Filled
Cakes

Turnovers

Cream-Filled
Sponge Cakes

Buttermilk Doughnuts

The tang of this batter makes these doughnuts an all-time favorite. You can glaze them as below or be a traditionalist and eat them plain.

2½ cups all-purpose flour

1 tsp. baking soda

½ tsp. baking powder

½ tsp. kosher salt

1 tsp. ground nutmeg (freshly grated)

1 cup buttermilk

1 egg

¼ cup (½ stick) unsalted butter, melted

1 recipe White Glaze (see Chapter 3)

Makes 15 to 20 doughnuts

Prep Time: 20 minutes

Cook Time: 30 minutes

1. In a large bowl, sift together flour, baking powder, baking soda, salt, and nutmeg.

2. In a separate bowl, whisk together buttermilk, egg, and butter. Add wet mixture to dry mixture and stir until just combined.

3. Turn onto a floured surface and knead three to five minutes until smooth.

4. In a heavy, deep frying pan, heat canola oil to 350°F.

5. Using a rolling pin, roll to ¼-inch thick and cut into shapes. Fry doughnuts in hot oil, one to two minutes on each side until evenly browned.

6. Drain on paper towels, then dip in White Glaze while hot.

Variation

◆ Decorate glaze with candy sprinkles, or try topping them with Chocolate Glaze instead.

Devil's Food Doughnuts

This batter is devilishly good, but it gets its name from the reddish color created when cocoa powder and baking soda are combined.

2½ cups cake flour

1 cup cocoa powder

2 tsp. baking soda

½ tsp. kosher salt

4 eggs

1½ cups sugar

⅓ cup buttermilk

3 TB. unsalted butter, melted

4-6 cups canola oil

1 recipe Ganache, glaze variation (see Chapter 3)

Makes 15 to 20 doughnuts

Prep Time: 20 minutes

Cook Time: 30 minutes, plus 1 hour cooling time

1. Sift together flour, cocoa, baking soda, and salt.

2. In a separate bowl, whisk together eggs, sugar, buttermilk, and melted butter. Add wet mixture to dry mixture and mix well. Chill one hour.

3. In a heavy, deep frying pan, heat canola oil to 350°F.

4. Turn dough onto a floured surface and knead briefly. Using a rolling pin, roll to ½-inch thick. Cut into shapes and fry doughnuts in hot oil, one to two minutes on each side until puffed and cooked through.

5. Drain on paper towels, then dip in ganache glaze and let stand until set, about five minutes.

Doughnut Holes

By their very nature, these doughnuts are leftovers. They are made from the center circle of dough removed during the cutting of traditional ring-shaped doughnuts. They cook faster, so keep an eye on them.

1 cup warm milk

1 (¼-oz.) pkg. active dry yeast

2 TB. sugar

¼ cup (½ stick) unsalted butter, melted

3 egg yolks

3 to 4 cups bread flour

1 tsp. kosher salt

1 tsp. cinnamon

1 recipe White Glaze (see Chapter 3)

Assorted toppings, including candy sprinkles, jimmies, chopped nuts, shredded coconut, and powdered sugar

> **Makes 15 to 20 doughnut holes**
>
> **Prep Time:** 90 minutes
>
> **Cook Time:** 30 minutes

1. Stir together milk, yeast, and sugar; and rest 10 minutes. Add butter, egg yolks, one cup flour, and salt and stir together to form a smooth paste. Add cinnamon and remaining flour to form a firm dough.

2. Transfer to a floured work surface and knead vigorously for 8 to 10 minutes until smooth and elastic. Return to bowl, dust with flour, cover with a warm, moist towel, and let rise until doubled in volume, about one hour.

3. In a heavy, deep frying pan, heat canola oil to 350°F.

4. Turn dough onto a floured surface, and with a rolling pin, roll to ¼-inch thick. Cut into two-inch circles and fry in hot oil, one to two minutes until evenly browned.

5. Drain on paper towels. While hot, dip into White Glaze, then dredge in desired topping. Let stand until set (about five minutes).

Jelly-Filled

1 cup warm milk

2 (¼-oz.) pkgs. active dry yeast

⅓ cup sugar

¼ cup (½ stick) unsalted butter, melted

3 egg yolks (reserve whites)

3 to 4 cups bread flour

1 tsp. kosher salt

2 cups fruit jam, preserves, or jelly

> **Makes 10 to 15 doughnuts**
>
> **Prep Time:** 90 minutes
>
> **Cook Time:** 30 minutes

1. Stir together milk, yeast, and sugar; rest 10 minutes. Add butter, egg yolks, one cup flour, and salt and stir together to form a smooth paste. Add remaining flour to form a firm dough.

2. Transfer to a floured work surface and knead vigorously for 8 to 10 minutes until smooth and elastic.

3. With a rolling pin, roll dough to ¼-inch thick and cut into three-inch circles. Place one to two teaspoons in the center of half the circles and brush the edges with egg white. Place remaining circles on top and press to seal edges.

4. Place on floured surface, dust tops lightly with flour, cover with a dry towel, and let rise until doubled in volume (about one hour).

5. In a heavy, deep frying pan, heat canola oil to 350°F. Fry in hot oil, two to three minutes per side until evenly browned. Drain on paper towels. Dust with powdered sugar while still hot.

Heads Up

Because these doughnuts are filled and have no hole, they will not cook as fast as the traditional shape. Cook a test doughnut first to gauge oil temperature and cooking time. When you think it's done, cut it open. If the dough is still runny in the center, reduce the oil temperature and lengthen the cooking time.

Old-Fashioned Doughnuts

Similar to Buttermilk Doughnuts with their tangy cake and crisp crust, the old-fashioned doughnut—plain or glazed—is an American favorite.

2 TB. unsalted butter

2 cups sugar, divided

2 eggs

2 tsp. vanilla extract

3½ cups all-purpose flour

4 tsp. baking powder

1 tsp. baking soda

½ tsp. kosher salt

1 cup sour cream

Makes 10 to 15 doughnuts

Prep Time: 30 minutes

Cook Time: 30 minutes, plus at least 3 hours cooling time

1. Beat together butter and one cup sugar until smooth. Add eggs and vanilla. Sift together flour, baking powder, baking soda, and salt; add alternately with sour cream.

2. Chill dough for at least three hours or overnight.

3. In a heavy, deep frying pan, heat canola oil to 350°F.

4. Turn onto a floured surface, knead briefly, and using a rolling pin roll to ½-inch thick. Cut into shapes and fry in hot oil one to two minutes on each side until evenly browned.

5. Drain on paper towels. While hot, dredge in remaining granulated sugar.

Powdered Sugar Doughnuts

These cakey, powdery treats are typically made in mini form—small enough to fit an entire one in your mouth.

3 eggs

1¼ cups sugar

1 cup sour cream

1 tsp. vanilla extract

4 cups all-purpose flour

1 tsp. baking soda

2 tsp. baking powder

½ tsp. kosher salt

3 cups powdered sugar, sifted

Makes 10 to 15 doughnuts

Prep Time: 30 minutes

Cook Time: 30 minutes, plus at least 3 hours cooling time

1. Combine eggs and sugar and whip until pale and fluffy, about three minutes. Add sour cream and vanilla. Sift together flour, baking soda, baking powder, and salt and stir into eggs.

2. Cover and chill at least three hours or overnight.

3. In a heavy, deep frying pan, heat canola oil to 350°F.

4. Turn dough onto a floured surface, knead briefly, then using a rolling pin roll to ½-inch thick. Cut into shapes and fry doughnuts in hot oil one to two minutes on each side until puffed and cooked through.

5. Drain on paper towels. Cool slightly, then dredge thoroughly in powdered sugar.

Raised Glazed Doughnuts

These holes of perfection are light and airy—a result of rich ingredients, vigorous kneading, and adequate *fermentation* time.

2 cups warm milk

2 (¼-oz.) pkgs. active dry yeast

½ cup sugar

¼ cup (½ stick) unsalted butter, melted

2 eggs

1 tsp. ground nutmeg

Zest of 1 lemon, grated finely

5 cups all-purpose flour

1 tsp. kosher salt

1 recipe White Glaze (see Chapter 3)

> **Makes 12 to 15 doughnuts**
>
> **Prep Time:** 30 minutes, plus 2 hours to rise
>
> **Cook Time:** 30 minutes

1. Stir together milk, yeast, and sugar and let rest 10 minutes. Add butter, egg, nutmeg, zest, one cup flour, and salt and stir together to form a smooth paste. Add remaining flour to form a firm dough.

2. Transfer to a floured work surface and knead vigorously for three to five minutes until smooth and elastic. Return to the bowl, dust with flour, cover with a warm, moist towel, and let rise until doubled in volume (about two hours).

3. In a heavy, deep frying pan, heat canola oil to 350°F.

4. Turn dough onto floured surface and pat with hands to ½-inch thick. Cut into shapes and fry in hot oil one to two minutes per side until evenly browned.

5. Drain on paper towels, and while hot, dip into White Glaze. Let stand until set (about five minutes).

Tidbits

Fermentation refers to the conversion of carbohydrates into alcohols and carbon dioxide. This process is usually referred to as "rising," and it takes a little longer when a dough is laden with fat. Be patient. When ready, the dough will be twice as big—and if you poke your finger into it, the hole will remain.

10

Cream Puffs

In This Chapter

◆ Classic pâte à choux dough

◆ Puffs, éclairs, and popovers

◆ Cold, creamy, light, and rich fillings

What's in a Name?

Cream puffs are made with a French dough called pâte à choux (pronounced pat-a-shoe). The name of this French batter is a little ambiguous. Pâte means dough or paste. Choux means cabbage. While at first glance it may seem to be named for its shape, cabbage is also a term of endearment in French—and these pastries are definitely something to be adored. So, the reasoning behind the name is a little unclear.

In addition to the cream puff, pâte à choux is the foundation of many classic pastries. But you would never know it at first glance. The heavy, eggy batter is gooey and sticky—not at all appetizing. But when pâte à choux hits the oven, this mess is transformed into pastry royalty.

The secret of this transformation is the eggs. Loaded with eggs means loaded with moisture. Moisture and heat have a short-lived relationship. When heated, moisture evaporates. The subsequent steam causes this batter to rise, or puff.

Getting It Right

There are several crucial stages of this dough's preparation. First, flour is added to water and cooked over heat for about three minutes. This time over the heat is important, giving the flour a chance to fully absorb the water and strengthening gluten proteins in the flour. When this step is cut short, the dough simply will not puff.

Next, eggs are added one by one off the heat. Each egg must be fully absorbed before the next is added. This not only keeps the task from making a sloppy counter mess but also gives your batter the correct consistency. This step is best done by hand. Excess friction from an electric mixer can easily turn your paste into soup. Batter that is too runny cannot be scooped into a mound, which is essential for baking a cream puff. If your batter should become runny through excess friction, it cannot be thickened by simply adding raw flour. Remember, the flour needs cooking and absorption time.

The process of stirring in the eggs can be strenuous, but it doesn't have to be done quickly. Take your time, and rest in between eggs if your arm begins to tire. Slow and steady wins the race.

Forming and Baking

The easiest way to form cream puffs is with an ice cream scoop. Not only is the shape perfect, but the scoop makes them uniform. Recipes in this chapter call for large or small puffs. Large should be about 1/4 to 1/3 cup of dough. Small puffs should be about 2 tablespoons of dough.

They can be any size you like as long you bake only one size per pan. Because the cooking time varies by size, multiple sizes per pan mean some will be overcooked and some undercooked.

To pan your puffs, line a baking sheet with parchment paper. Because this dough is so gooey, chefs often use a smudge of dough in each corner of the paper to glue it to the pan. This keeps the paper from moving around as you try to scoop or pipe your dough. Space your choux so it has ample room to grow, with at least two inches between items.

Baking pâte à choux should be done at fairly high temperatures. The high burst of heat encourages the quick production of steam. Be sure to keep the puffs in the oven until they are a deep golden brown. If they are too blonde, the batter is not set; they will be eggy inside, and the puffs will fall.

Pâte à Choux

This classic recipe is a standard skill for all pastry chefs. But don't let that intimidate you. Once you try it, you'll be hooked.

2 cups water

5 oz. (1¼ sticks) unsalted butter

1 TB. sugar

1 tsp. kosher salt

1⅔ cups all-purpose flour

7 eggs

1 egg yolk

> **Makes about 1 quart of batter, enough for 1 dozen large puffs or 2 dozen smaller puffs**
>
> **Prep Time:** 10 minutes
>
> **Cook Time:** 90 minutes

To Make Batter:

1. Preheat the oven to 400°F. Coat a baking sheet with nonstick cooking spray.

2. In a large saucepan, combine water, butter, sugar, and salt and bring to a boil. At the boil, add flour and stir vigorously with a sturdy spoon for at least three minutes until all flour is absorbed and mixture resembles mashed potatoes.

3. Remove from heat and cool slightly.

4. Add eggs one at a time, blending each one thoroughly before adding the next. Once eggs are in, this batter can be used for a number of recipes, including cheese puffs, éclairs, and even the croquembouche.

5. Batter cannot be stored refrigerated for more than an hour or two uncooked before it starts to discolor.

To Make Puffs:

1. Preheat the oven to 400°F. Line a baking sheet with parchment paper.

2. Using an ice cream scoop, scoop dough, scrape scooper against rim of pan to flatten the base, and evenly space on prepared pan.

3. Make an egg wash with egg yolk and cream; brush lightly on top of each puff.

4. Bake at 400°F until puffed and golden brown, about 15 minutes, then
    reduce heat to 325°F and bake until firm and dark brown, about 10
    minutes more. Cool completely, then finish according to the follow-
    ing recipes.

Variation

◆ **Éclairs:** Using a pastry bag fitted with a large, plain tip, pipe choux
    dough into thick cylinders, about 1×4 inches. Draw the tines of a
    fork down the length of the éclair before egg washing and baking
    to encourage puffing. Bake as you would cream puffs.

Helpful Hints

Pâte à choux can be baked into shape in advance and frozen for
up to a week. To use, spread frozen puffs on a baking sheet in a
single layer, then bake for 10 minutes at 350°F to refresh.

Chocolate Cream Puffs

This filling is a classic *chocolate mousse*. Light but rich, it makes a decadent treat. You can jazz it up with some fresh berries, orange segments, or caramel sauce hidden under the mousse at the base of the puff.

8-10 large Pâte à Choux cream puffs, tops removed

1 cup bittersweet chocolate chips

2 TB. unsalted butter

2 TB. espresso or strong coffee

1 cup cream

3 eggs, separated

1 TB. sugar

1 recipe Ganache, glaze variation (see Chapter 3)

Serves 8 to 10
Prep Time: 45 minutes, plus 90 minutes to make choux puffs

1. Combine chocolate, butter, and coffee in the top of a double boiler set over medium heat. Stir over simmering water until melted. Remove from heat; set aside to cool.

2. Whip cream to medium peaks, then refrigerate. Whip whites to medium peaks, slowly add sugar, then continue whipping to stiffen peaks. Set aside.

3. In a large bowl, whip egg yolks until pale and light, about three minutes. Slowly add warm chocolate mixture while whipping.

4. Fold in half of cream, all egg whites, then remaining cream.

5. Fill each puff generously with chocolate mousse, replace tops, and drizzle with ganache glaze.

6. Chill 15 minutes to set. Dust with cocoa powder before serving.

Sweet Talk

Chocolate mousse is not from Minnesota. In French, mousse means foam—and in culinary terms, it denotes anything that has been lightened with air.

Chocolate Éclairs

Éclairs are essentially long cream puffs with a custard filling. For this recipe, be sure to stick with bittersweet chocolate. Milk or white chocolate is too pale and will turn this custard into an unappealing grayish-brown color.

4 egg yolks

1 cup sugar

⅓ cup cornstarch

4 cups half-and-half

1 TB. vanilla extract

2 oz. bittersweet chocolate

2 TB. butter

8-10 pâte à choux éclairs

1 recipe Ganache, glaze variation (see Chapter 3)

Serves 8 to 10
Prep Time: 40 minutes, plus 90 minutes to make choux éclairs

1. In a small bowl, whisk together egg yolks, sugar, and cornstarch; set aside.

2. In a large saucepan, combine half-and-half and vanilla and bring to a boil over high heat. At the boil, ladle ½ cup of hot half-and-half into the yolks and whisk quickly to combine.

3. Pour warmed yolks into the saucepan, and over high heat whisk immediately and vigorously until mixture begins to resemble thick sour cream, about two minutes.

4. Remove from heat; add chocolate and butter and stir to combine. Strain into a large bowl and cover with plastic wrap pressed directly on the surface. Chill completely.

5. With a paring knife, poke two holes in the bottom of each éclair about one inch from each end.

6. Fit a pastry bag with a small plain pastry tip and fill the bag with chocolate pastry cream. Insert tip and inject cream until you feel the éclair expanding. Repeat with all éclairs.

7. Invert and dip tops in ganache glaze and chill 15 minutes to set. Dust with powdered sugar before serving.

Coffee Cream Puffs

This is a simplified version of a classic French cream puff called a *religeuse*. The caramel color is said to be an homage to an order of nuns who donned brown habits.

1 recipe Sweetened Whipped Cream, Coffee Cream variation (see Chapter 3)

8-10 large pâte à choux puffs, tops removed

1 recipe Caramel Sauce (see Chapter 3)

Serves 8 to 10
Prep Time: 30 minutes, plus 90 minutes to make choux éclairs

1. Fit a pastry bag with a large star pastry tip. Fill the bag half full with coffee cream and pipe into the bottom of each puff, mounding it up above the edge.

2. Replace tops, drizzle with caramel sauce, and serve immediately.

Profiteroles

Cream puffs of all kinds are often mistakenly called profiteroles. But the real thing consists of three vanilla ice cream–filled choux puffs drizzled with chocolate. Simple and elegant.

12-18 small Pâte à Choux puffs

1 quart vanilla ice cream

1 recipe Ganache, glaze variation (see Chapter 3)

¼ cup powdered sugar

Serves 4 to 6
Prep Time: 20 minutes, plus 90 minutes to make choux éclairs

1. Slice each small puff in half. Fill each puff with a small, round scoop of vanilla ice cream.

2. Replace the puff's top and store in the freezer until ready to serve.

3. Place three puffs on each plate, drizzle with warm ganache glaze, dust with powdered sugar, and serve immediately.

Cream-Filled Swans

These cute pastries are a standard fare on European-style dessert buffets. They are easy to make and always result in a smile. If you serve them on a mirror, they look like they're swimming.

1 recipe pâte à choux puffs

1 recipe Sweetened Whipped Cream (see Chapter 3)

1 pint strawberries, washed and sliced

¼ cup powdered sugar

Serves 6 to 8

Prep Time: 30 minutes, plus 90 minutes to make choux puffs

1. Preheat the oven to 400°F. Line two baking sheets with parchment paper.

2. Fit a pastry bag with a large star pastry tip. Fill bag with pâte à choux dough and pipe into eight large teardrop shapes. These will be the swan bodies.

3. Reserve one cup batter and transfer to a pastry bag fitted with a small plain tip.

4. On a separate baking sheet, pipe eight large S-shapes. These will be the swan heads and necks.

5. Brush with egg wash and bake.

6. Remove necks when golden brown, about 10 minutes.

7. Reduce heat to 350°F and continue cooking bodies for another 30 to 40 minutes until dark golden brown. Cool completely.

8. Cut the top third off each swan body and set the top of the puff aside.

9. Place a few sliced strawberries into the base of the swan body, then pipe or spoon whipped cream on top.

10. Cut the top of the puff in half lengthwise and insert upright into cream, forming the wings. Insert necks and dust with powdered sugar before serving.

Vanilla Cream Puffs

These classic puffs are filled with a rich vanilla custard. When made smaller and stacked in a pyramid held together by caramel, they become a *croquembouche*.

4 egg yolks

1 cup sugar

$\frac{1}{3}$ cup cornstarch

4 cups half-and-half

$\frac{1}{2}$ vanilla bean

1 TB. vanilla extract

2 TB. butter

8-10 large Pâte à Choux puffs

1 recipe Ganache, glaze variation (see Chapter 3)

Serves 8 to 10
Prep Time: 40 minutes, plus 90 minutes to make choux puffs

1. In a small bowl, whisk together egg yolks, sugar, and cornstarch; set aside.

2. In a large saucepan, combine half-and-half and vanilla extract; bring to a boil over high heat.

3. Split vanilla bean down the center, scrape seeds out with a paring knife, and add them to the half-and-half. At the boil, ladle $\frac{1}{2}$ cup hot half-and-half into yolks and whisk quickly to combine.

4. Pour warmed yolks into the saucepan, and over high heat whisk immediately and vigorously until mixture begins to resemble thick sour cream, about one minute.

5. Remove from heat, add butter, and stir to combine. Strain into a large bowl, cover with plastic wrap pressed directly on the surface, and chill completely.

6. With a paring knife, poke a hole in the bottom of each puff.

7. Fit a pastry bag with a small plain pastry tip and fill the bag with cooled vanilla cream. Insert tip and inject cream until you feel the puff expanding. Repeat with all puffs.

8. Dip puff tops into ganache glaze, invert onto a plate, and chill to set. Dust with powdered sugar before serving.

Sweet Talk

A **croquembouche** is a classic French wedding pastry that consists of 50, 100, or more small vanilla custard-filled pâte à choux puffs glued together with hot caramel. The entire thing is wrapped with golden spun sugar and is often placed on a base made of caramelized nuts called *nougatine*.

Chocolate Chip Popovers

Popovers are very similar to pâte à choux puffs in their texture and flavor. The batter is a little easier, but you have little control over the final shape. (And that doesn't matter, as you won't be looking at them for long.)

4 eggs, room temperature

2 cups milk, room temperature

2 cups all-purpose flour

1 tsp. kosher salt

1 cup chocolate chips (use mini chips if available)

Serves 12
Prep Time: 30 minutes
Cook Time: 35 minutes

1. Preheat the oven to 400°F. Place the popover pan into the oven to heat up as well.

2. Combine eggs, milk, flour, salt, and chocolate chips in a blender. Blend until well combined.

3. Pour batter into the pan, filling each cup to the rim.

4. Bake 15 minutes at 400°F, then turn the heat down to 375°F and bake another 20 minutes until golden brown.

5. Serve immediately.

Helpful Hints

Temperature is the key to good popovers. Be sure the ingredients have lost their chill from the refrigerator, be sure you have a real popover pan (you can find one through the resources in Appendix B), be sure to preheat your pan, and don't open the oven door during the first 30 minutes of baking. If you do, the temperature will drop dramatically and the popovers will fall.

Chapter 11

Sweet Rolls

In This Chapter

◆ Classic puff pastry and Danish dough

◆ Yeasted sweet dough

◆ Delectable pastries in all shapes and sizes

Scratch It

Baking from scratch is as satisfying as it gets. Freed from the boxed mixes and the popping-fresh premade dough, you discover that the real flavor of baked goods is so much better than anything you can buy at the market.

But besides the rise in quality, your from-scratch baking offers a sense of accomplishment. Turning raw ingredients into a delicious pastry is guaranteed to make your family smile and make you feel like a million bucks. That's because there is little in life more satisfying than the completion of a challenging task.

In baking, there are few challenges as satisfying as puff pastry. But once you try it, you open an entirely new world of scratch baking.

Laminated Dough

The secret to puff pastry is the lamination. Laminated dough is dough with tightly compacted, alternating layers. In the case of puff pastry, the layers are dough and butter. Without these layers, there will be no puff. The key is in the butter.

Butter contains a large amount of water. When the butter hits the heat of the oven, the water evaporates into steam—and the steam pushes the dough layers up. It is the same principle employed in pâte à choux dough (see Chapter 10).

Turning

To get those many layers, butter is encased in dough and the entire mass is rolled out into a sheet. Then, through a series of rolling, folding, and refrigeration, the layers increase to several hundred. Throughout this process (known as turning), the dough and butter should remain cold but not so cold that it becomes brittle. This determination can only be made by the baker, however, because refrigerators, kitchens, seasons, and parts of the world all vary in temperature.

The basic turn is called a *single turn*, and it is essentially a business letter fold. The dough is rolled into a large rectangle. That rectangle is divided visually into thirds, and each end is folded toward the other. This process is repeated several times, with refrigeration in between to keep the butter and dough cool and easy to handle. Throughout the process, remember that refrigeration and flour are your friends. Work quickly to keep the dough cold, and have patience.

Problems may arise if the rolling squeezes some butter out of the dough and onto your counter. It is not uncommon and is easily remedied. Just douse the butter with flour, tuck it back in, and pretend it didn't happen. Try not to roll over that spot again. Fold it inward on the next turn, and let it chill to solidify.

Sweet Dough

Any dough that has sugar in it can be termed sweet dough, but in the realm of baking, the term generally refers to yeast dough enriched with butter, eggs, and sugar. Such doughs are used to create all sorts of products, including cinnamon rolls, brioche, dumplings, and a plethora of holiday fruit breads around the world.

Unlike yeast dough for French bread or pizza (known as lean dough, or dough with little fat), sweet dough has a tighter crumb and takes a little longer to rise. These factors are a result of the excess fat and sugar, which is heavy and therefore harder for yeast-produced carbon dioxide to lift. Be patient when waiting for the volume to double. It's worth the effort, I promise!

Forming Pastries

Both laminated and sweet dough are loaded with butter, and butter warms up quickly. Therefore, it is important to keep the dough cold when trying to cut and form it. You may find it necessary to return it to the refrigerator from time to time to let the fat solidify. You'll know when that time comes because your dough will start to stick, and it will be difficult to maintain shapes when moving it from work surface to baking sheet.

Classic Puff Pastry

1 cup unsalted butter

1 tsp. lemon juice

2 cups all-purpose flour

$\frac{1}{2}$ tsp. kosher salt

$\frac{1}{2}$ to $\frac{3}{4}$ cup ice water

> **Makes about**
> **1$\frac{1}{4}$ lb. of dough**
>
> **Prep Time:** About 4 hours

1. Beat cold butter until it is creamy and lump free. Form into a four-inch disc and refrigerate.

2. Sift flour into a large bowl; add salt and $\frac{1}{4}$ cup water. Stir together with a fork, slowly adding more water as needed until it just comes together into soft dough. Chill for 30 minutes.

3. Working on a floured surface, pat dough into a six-inch circle. Place butter on top and wrap dough over, completely encasing butter. Dust with flour, turn over, and with a rolling pin using short, light motion, roll into a rectangle $\frac{1}{2}$-inch thick. Make a single turn and refrigerate 30 minutes.

4. Remove chilled dough from the refrigerator. Place on a floured surface and roll again into a rectangle $\frac{1}{2}$-inch thick using short, light motions. Make another single turn and refrigerate. Repeat this process for a total of six single turns, chilling between each. After the last turn, roll to $\frac{1}{4}$-inch thick. The puff pastry is now ready for use or storage. Wrap it airtight and refrigerate for 24 hours, or freeze for up to two weeks.

Helpful Hints

If you're short on time, use frozen puff pastry for these recipes. The finished product is less delectable but also less hassle. Keep in mind that mass-produced puff pastry is usually made with partially hydrogenated vegetable oil (also known as trans fat), which is generally unhealthy and leaves behind an unpleasant aftertaste.

Sweet Dough

This dough is a basic recipe that can be used for dozens of pastries. Use it for the recipes in this chapter, then come up with some of your own ideas.

1 cup warm milk

2 (¼-oz.) pkg. active dry yeast

1 tsp. honey

¼ cup sugar

½ cup (1 stick) unsalted butter

3 eggs

3 to 4 cups bread flour

1 tsp. kosher salt

> **Makes about 12 to 15 pastries**
>
> **Prep Time:** 45 minutes, plus about 4 hours for Danish dough
>
> **Cook Time:** 20 minutes

1. In a large bowl, combine milk, yeast, and honey. Stir and set aside 10 minutes.

2. Add sugar, butter, eggs, and one cup flour and beat until smooth. Add salt and enough remaining flour to create soft dough.

3. Turn onto a floured surface and knead vigorously for 8 to 10 minutes until dough is smooth and elastic.

4. Cover with a warm, moist towel and set aside to double in volume, about two hours. After dough has doubled, it can be used or wrapped airtight and refrigerated up to 12 hours.

Heads Up

When making yeast dough, the yeast needs warmth to begin fermentation. But if it gets too warm or hot, the yeast will die. There is no need for a thermometer, though. The liquid needs to be only slightly warmer than body temperature. If you can hold your finger in it and it feels warm, that's perfect.

Danish Dough

This dough is essentially the same as puff pastry, but it has yeast. The yeast in the dough portion of this laminate gives a unique and delicious flavor.

1¼ cups unsalted butter

1 tsp. lemon juice

1¼ cups milk, warmed

1 (¼-oz.) envelope active dry yeast

2 TB. sugar

1 tsp. ground cardamom

1 egg

1 tsp. kosher salt

2 to 3 cups all-purpose flour

Makes about 1¼ lb. of dough
Prep Time: About 4 hours

1. Beat cold butter until creamy and lump free. Form into a four-inch disc and refrigerate.

2. Combine milk, yeast, and sugar in a large bowl and set aside 10 minutes. Add cardamom, egg, salt, and one cup flour and beat into a batter. Slowly add flour as needed until it just comes together into soft dough. Wrap well and chill for 30 minutes.

3. Working on a floured surface, pat dough into a six-inch circle. Place butter on top and wrap dough over, completely encasing butter. Dust with flour, turn over, and with a rolling pin using short, light motions, roll into a rectangle ½-inch thick. Make a *single turn*, and refrigerate 30 minutes.

4. Remove chilled dough from the refrigerator, place on a floured surface, and roll again into a rectangle ½-inch thick using short, light motions. Make another single turn and refrigerate. Repeat this process for a total of six single turns, chilling between each. After the last turn, roll to ¼-inch thick.

5. The dough is now ready for use or storage. Wrap it airtight and refrigerate for 24 hours, or freeze for up to two weeks.

Apple Turnovers

The apples you use are a matter of preference. In this application, all apples will cook the same. The best advice is to use what you like to eat! If it's good in your lunch box, it will be good in your turnover.

3 TB. unsalted butter

8 apples, peeled and sliced

¼ cup brown sugar

1 tsp. cinnamon

½ tsp. kosher salt

1 recipe Classic Puff Pastry

1 egg

1 cup sugar

> **Makes about 12 to 15 turnovers**
>
> **Prep Time:** 30 minutes, plus about 4 hours for puff pastry
>
> **Cook Time:** 20 minutes

1. Melt butter in a large sauté pan over high heat. Add apples, sugar, cinnamon, and salt and toss to coat. Reduce heat to medium and cook until tender and golden brown, about 20 minutes. Cool completely.

2. Preheat the oven to 375°F. Line two baking sheets with parchment paper.

3. Roll out puff pastry dough to ¼-inch thick and cut into four-inch squares.

4. Combine egg with a tablespoon of water and brush along each edge of square. Place one tablespoon cooled apples in the center of each square, then fold dough over to create a triangle. Seal edges and place on the prepared pan. Repeat with remaining dough.

5. Brush each turnover with remaining egg wash, sprinkle with sugar, and bake until puffed and golden brown (about 20 minutes). Cool before serving.

 Heads Up _____

Measure carefully and cut your laminated dough efficiently, to minimize waste. Carefully layered scraps cannot be gathered and rerolled because all the layers will be lost.

Bear Claws

These buttery, almond-filled pastries are meant to resemble a bear's claw. That's some delicious bear!

1 (7-oz.) pkg. almond paste

$\frac{1}{2}$ cup (1 stick) unsalted butter

$1\frac{1}{2}$ cups graham cracker crumbs

1 tsp. ground nutmeg

$\frac{1}{4}$ to $\frac{1}{2}$ cup Simple Syrup (see Chapter 3)

1 recipe Danish Dough

1 egg

$\frac{1}{2}$ cup sugar

> **Makes about 12 to 15 bear claws**
>
> **Prep Time:** 45 minutes, plus about 4 hours for Danish dough
>
> **Cook Time:** 20 minutes

1. Preheat the oven to 375°F. Line two baking sheets with parchment paper.

2. Beat together almond paste and butter until smooth and creamy. Add graham cracker crumbs and nutmeg and mix well. Slowly drizzle in enough Simple Syrup to create a soft paste.

3. Roll out Danish dough to $\frac{1}{4}$-inch thick and cut into 4×6-inch rectangles. Combine egg with a tablespoon of water and brush along each edge of rectangle. Place two tablespoons of almond filling down the center length of each rectangle.

4. Fold dough over to create a 2×6-inch rectangle. Press to seal, and with a sharp knife make small slits every inch along sealed edge.

5. Transfer to the prepared pan and bend bear claw into a horseshoe so that the slits open up, creating "claws." Repeat with remaining dough.

6. Brush each pastry with remaining egg wash, sprinkle with sugar, and bake until puffed and golden brown (about 20 minutes). Cool before serving.

Cinnamon Buns

This is a great recipe to make when you want to impress someone. Anyone who enters your house when it is filled with the aroma of these baking buns will be your friend for life.

1 cup sugar

3 TB. cinnamon

1 recipe Sweet Dough

¼ cup (½ stick) unsalted butter, melted

1 egg

¼ tsp. kosher salt

1 recipe White Glaze (see Chapter 3)

> **Makes about 12 to 15 pastries**
>
> **Prep Time:** 60 minutes, plus about 3 hours for sweet dough
>
> **Cook Time:** 20 minutes

1. Line two baking sheets with parchment paper. Combine cinnamon and sugar; set aside.

2. Turn dough onto a floured surface, and with a rolling pin roll into an 18×24-inch rectangle. Brush entire surface with melted butter, then generously sprinkle with cinnamon sugar.

3. Starting on a long edge, roll the dough into a log. Slice log into two-inch wheels. Space wheels two inches apart on the prepared pan, dust lightly with flour, cover with plastic wrap, and set aside to rise for 30 minutes.

4. Preheat the oven to 350°F.

5. In a small bowl, make an egg wash by combining the egg, salt, and water. Brush on top of the rolls and bake until golden brown and firm, about 15 minutes. Cool 10 minutes, then drizzle with White Glaze.

Variation:

◆ You can omit the White Glaze and top these rolls with a simple dusting of powdered sugar or go all-out and frost them with Cream Cheese Icing (see Chapter 3).

Cinnamon Raisin Snails

This recipe is similar to cinnamon buns, but the Danish dough turns it into a completely different item. Buttery and flaky, these are snails that the kids won't mind eating.

1 cup sugar

3 TB. cinnamon

1 recipe Danish Dough

¼ cup (½ stick) unsalted butter, melted

1 cup raisins

1 egg

¼ tsp. kosher salt

1 cup Simple Syrup (see Chapter 3)

> **Makes about 12 to 15 snails**
>
> **Prep Time:** 60 minutes, plus about 4 hours for Danish dough
>
> **Cook Time:** 20 minutes

1. Line two baking sheets with parchment paper. Combine cinnamon and sugar; set aside.

2. Turn dough onto a floured surface, and with a rolling pin roll into a rectangle at least 18×24 inches. Brush entire surface with melted butter, then sprinkle generously with cinnamon sugar and raisins.

3. Starting on a long edge, roll the dough into a log. Slice log into two-inch wheels. Space wheels two inches apart on the prepared pan, dust lightly with flour, cover with plastic wrap, and set aside to rise for 30 minutes.

4. Preheat the oven to 350°F.

5. In a small bowl, make an egg wash by combining the egg, salt, and water. Brush on top of snails and bake them until golden brown and firm, about 15 minutes.

6. Immediately brush each snail lightly with Simple Syrup, then cool.

Palmiers

Sometimes called elephant ears, these flat, crisp cookies are loaded with buttery goodness. Be sure to let them cool completely before you dig in to give them a chance to fully crisp.

1 recipe puff pastry

2 to 3 cups sugar

1 cup Simple Syrup (see Chapter 3)

> **Makes about
> 15 to 20 Palmiers**
>
> **Prep Time:** 20 minutes, plus about 4 hours for puff pastry
>
> **Cook Time:** 20 minutes

1. Line two baking sheets with parchment paper.

2. Turn dough onto a floured surface, and with a rolling pin roll into an 18×24-inch rectangle. Cover entire surface generously with sugar, reserving one cup.

3. Fold edges toward the center until they just meet. Top with more sugar, then repeat, giving dough four layers. Top with sugar again, fold in half like a book, and chill at least one hour.

4. Preheat the oven to 350°F.

5. Slice the log into ¹/₂-inch "heart"-shaped cookies. Dredge each cookie generously in sugar and space wheels two inches apart on the prepared pan.

6. Bake 10 minutes until dough begins to set, then flip with a spatula and bake until golden brown, about 10 minutes more. Cool completely before serving.

 Heads Up _____

> Watch these carefully. They are thin and can burn quickly with all that sugar. Rotate the pan if necessary to promote even browning.

Sticky Buns

These are nothing more than upside-down cinnamon rolls with a gooey bottom that becomes the top. You can bake them in muffin tins (as we do here) or bake them together in a cake pan.

1 cup brown sugar

2 TB. honey

10 oz. (2½ sticks) butter, softened and divided

¼ cup milk

2 TB. flour

2 cups chopped pecans

1 recipe Sweet Dough

1 cup sugar

3 TB. cinnamon

> **Makes about 10 sticky buns**
>
> **Prep Time:** 60 minutes, plus 3 hours for Sweet Dough
>
> **Cook Time:** 30 minutes

1. Generously coat three muffin tins with nonstick cooking spray.

2. Mix together brown sugar, honey, two sticks butter, milk, flour, and nuts into a paste. Divide paste evenly between the muffin cups.

3. Melt remaining butter.

4. Turn dough onto a floured surface, and with a rolling pin roll into a 9×40-inch rectangle. Brush entire surface with melted butter. Combine cinnamon and sugar and sprinkle evenly over butter.

5. Starting on a long edge, roll dough into a log. Slice log into three-inch wheels and place in each muffin cup. Dust lightly with flour, cover with plastic wrap, and set aside to rise for 30 minutes.

6. Preheat the oven to 350°F.

7. Bake buns for 15 to 20 minutes until golden brown and bubbly. Remove from oven, cool 10 minutes, and while still warm, carefully invert onto a serving platter. Cool before serving.

Heads Up

Remember, hot sugar burns badly. Use oven mitts and caution when inverting the sticky buns. That topping is like lava.

Part 5

Small Cakes

This portion of recipes is dedicated to the "mini-me" of the snack world. Stuffed, rolled, or sandwiched, these recipes are guaranteed to put a smile on your face.

Classic fruitcakes, coffee cakes, crumb cakes, and even pies are all represented in diminutive form. It is these cakes, with their attention to detail and personalized presentation, that really let your baking skills shine. What could be more impressive than a tiny lemon meringue pie or a homemade cream-filled mini sponge cake?

Chapter 12

Mini Cakes

In This Chapter

- ◆ Fruity and nutty cakes
- ◆ Cream-filled cakes
- ◆ Familiar favorites

What's more fun than cake? Mini cakes, that's what. Nothing says "I care about you" more than the presentation of an individually sized morsel of cakey goodness.

Of course, mini cakes are merely the offspring of regular, grown-up cakes. Consequently, all of these recipes can be baked in a larger version if you like.

Adjusting for Size

Cakes in smaller pans can bake at a higher temperature than cakes in big pans. Heat needs time to penetrate the batter, and if a cake is too big and the temperature is too high, the outer cake will overcook before the center is done. To be safe, lower the temperature by 25°F when baking a big cake based on a small-cake recipe.

A change in temperature means a change in bake time, too. Larger cakes can take anywhere from 30 minutes to an hour or more to bake properly. Pans with holes in the center, such as bundt pans or angel food cake pans, are a touch quicker because heat can penetrate from the center as well as from the side. It's best to check often.

Tidbits

If you'd like to bake a large cake in a smaller version as we have done in this chapter, simply increase the temperature by 25°F. The added heat speeds the rate at which the chemical leaveners react, and the cakes will rise high.

You can tell that a cake is done when you touch the top. If it feels firm and springs right back, it's ready. If your finger leaves a mark, it needs more time. You can try the skewer test (where a skewer inserted in the center comes out clean when done), but it doesn't work on all batters. Another method is to look at the side of the pan. Finished cakes contract, leaving a little space between the cake and the pan.

Mini Pans

Today, cookware stores are crammed to the ceilings with cute and fancy bakeware. Pans come in every shape imaginable and are made from a plethora of materials, including nonstick, cast iron, and even silicone. The choice is yours. Appendix B has a list of resources to stock your bakeware cabinet.

If you bake your mini cakes in muffin pans, put the batter in paper cups so that when they are baked, it will be easier to get them out. If your mini pan is not muffin-shaped, it is unlikely you will find papers to fit. In that case, use nonstick cooking spray generously and give yourself cake-release insurance by dusting with flour. Fill each pan with flour, swirl it around to be sure it is totally coated, then firmly tap out the excess.

Fillings

Many of these mini cakes are based on some all-time store-bought favorites. However, many of the fillings you find in your store are based on shortening made with partially hydrogenated vegetable oils, or trans fat. The recipes in this chapter use the fillings from Chapter 3, which are all made with butter. You'll find the flavor so exceptional that you may never buy cake at a convenience store again.

There are two ways to get frosting into the center of a cake. A small plug can be cut from the center, then replaced once the cavity is filled with frosting. This method is ideal when the cut area can be iced over and decorated. The filling also can be injected using a pastry bag. This method goes a little more quickly and is recommended when you have many cakes to fill.

Cream Cheese Pound Cakes

The key to these rich pound cakes is in the beating. Dense with butter, they rely on air beaten in to raise them up. If you have an electric mixer, now is a good time to use it.

1½ cups (3 sticks) unsalted butter

2 cups sugar

1 cup brown sugar

1 (8-oz.) pkg. cream cheese, softened

6 eggs

1 TB. vanilla extract

½ tsp. kosher salt

3 cups cake flour

Makes 6 mini cakes
Prep Time: 20 minutes
Cook Time: 25 minutes

1. Preheat the oven to 350°F. Coat six mini loaf pans with nonstick cooking spray.

2. Beat butter and sugar together until smooth and creamy. Add cream cheese and continue beating until well incorporated. Add eggs one by one, then add vanilla and salt.

3. Sift flour and add slowly until fully incorporated.

4. Transfer to prepared pans, filling ¾ full. Bake until golden brown and firm to the touch, about 20 to 25 minutes. Cool cakes 10 minutes, and while still warm, invert to remove from pans.

Tidbits

Before baking powder, air and yeast were the only leavening agents available to bakers. For non-yeasted cakes, elbow grease was a must. Those ladies must have had serious upper-arm muscles!

Sour Lemon Pound Cakes

Because we have a fruitful lemon tree in our yard, this cake has become a family favorite. For a tropical twist, try making this recipe with key limes.

1 cup (2 sticks) unsalted butter

1½ cups sugar

Zest and juice of 4 lemons, separated

4 eggs

3 cups cake flour

2 tsp. baking powder

½ tsp. kosher salt

1 cup milk

2 cups Simple Syrup (see Chapter 3)

Makes 6 mini cakes
Prep Time: 20 minutes
Cook Time: 25 minutes

1. Preheat the oven to 350°F. Coat six mini bundt pans with nonstick cooking spray.

2. Beat butter, sugar, and lemon zest together until smooth and creamy. Add eggs one by one.

3. Sift together flour, baking powder, and salt and add alternately with milk.

4. Transfer to prepared pans, filling ¾ full. Bake until golden brown and firm to the touch, about 20 to 25 minutes.

5. Combine lemon juice and Simple Syrup; set aside.

6. Cool cakes 10 minutes, and while still warm, invert to remove from pans.

7. Immediately drizzle cakes with lemon syrup and cool completely.

Peanut Butter-Filled Chocolate Cake

There is no better-loved culinary pair than peanut butter and chocolate. Don't they make a sweet couple?

4 cups cake flour

1 cup cocoa powder

1 TB. plus 1½ tsp. baking soda

½ tsp. kosher salt

3 eggs

2⅔ cups sugar

1 cup canola oil

1½ cups buttermilk

1½ cups strong brewed coffee

1 recipe White Frosting (see Chapter 3)

1 cup peanut butter

1 recipe Ganache, glaze variation (see
Chapter 3)

Makes 6 mini cakes
Prep Time: 20 minutes
Cook Time: 25 minutes
Finishing Time: 30 minutes

1. Preheat the oven to 350°F. Coat six mini loaf pans with nonstick
   cooking spray.

2. Sift together flour, cocoa powder, baking soda, and salt; set aside.

3. In a large bowl, whip together eggs and sugar until fluffy and pale
   yellow, about five minutes. Combine oil, buttermilk, and coffee and
   add alternately with dry ingredients. Transfer to prepared pans, filling ¾ full. Bake until set but springy to the touch, about 20 to 25
   minutes. Cool completely.

4. Fold together White Frosting and peanut butter.

5. Use a chopstick to make a hole at each end of each cake. Fit a pastry
   bag with a small plain pastry tip. Fill the bag with frosting, insert
   the tip, and inject until you feel the cake expanding. Repeat with all
   cakes.

6. Drizzle with ganache glaze and chill again briefly to set before
   serving.

Golden Gingerbread

Slightly more elegant than dark-brown gingerbread, this one has a lighter, more buttery crumb.

½ cup (1 stick) unsalted butter

1 cup brown sugar

2 eggs

1 tsp. vanilla extract

⅓ cup sour cream

⅔ cup buttermilk

2¼ cups cake flour

1 tsp. baking soda

1 tsp. baking powder

½ tsp. kosher salt

1 TB. ground ginger

1 tsp. ground cardamom

½ tsp. ground cinnamon

½ tsp. ground nutmeg

1 cup golden raisins

1 recipe Vanilla Frosting (see Chapter 3)

2 TB. molasses

Makes 6 mini cakes
Prep Time: 20 minutes
Cook Time: 25 minutes

1. Preheat the oven to 350°F. Coat six mini loaf pans with nonstick cooking spray.

2. Beat butter and sugar together until smooth and creamy. Add eggs one by one, then add vanilla.

3. Combine sour cream and buttermilk; set aside.

4. Sift together flour, baking powder, baking soda, salt, ginger, cardamom, cinnamon, and nutmeg and add alternately with buttermilk. Fold in raisins.

5. Transfer to prepared pans, filling ³/₄ full. Bake until golden brown and firm to the touch, about 20 to 25 minutes.

6. Combine White Frosting and molasses; set aside.

7. Cool cakes 10 minutes, and while still warm, invert to remove from pans. Immediately drizzle cakes with molasses glaze; cool completely.

Trail Mix Cakes

These sound healthy, until you realize they're loaded with M&M's. They do pack a hefty amount of energy, perfect when you peter out on your next hike.

2 cups all-purpose flour

¼ cup whole-wheat flour

2 tsp. baking powder

½ tsp. kosher salt

1 cup granola

2 eggs

¾ cup brown sugar

1 cup milk

¾ cup canola oil

1 tsp. vanilla

½ cup dry-roasted peanuts

½ cup raisins

1 cup M&Ms

1 recipe Ganache, glaze variation (see Chapter 3)

Makes 6 mini cakes
Prep Time: 20 minutes
Cook Time: 20 minutes

1. Preheat the oven to 375°F. Coat six mini bundt pans with nonstick cooking spray.

2. In a large bowl, sift together all-purpose flour, whole-wheat flour, baking powder, and salt. Stir in granola.

3. In a separate bowl, blend thoroughly eggs, sugar, milk, oil, and vanilla, then stir into dry ingredients until just combined. Fold in peanuts, raisins, and M&Ms.

4. Transfer batter to prepared pans, filling ¾ full. Bake until golden brown and firm, about 20 to 25 minutes. Cool cakes 10 minutes, and while still warm, invert to remove from pans. Immediately drizzle cakes with ganache and cool completely.

Coconut Cream-Filled Cakes

These cakes are the definition of fun. You can make them with coconut *au naturel*, or add red food coloring for a pink version.

2 cups all-purpose flour

1 TB. baking powder

$\frac{1}{2}$ tsp. kosher salt

$\frac{1}{2}$ cup shortening

1 cup sugar

4 egg whites

1 TB. coconut extract, divided

$\frac{1}{2}$ cup evaporated milk

1 recipe Vanilla Frosting (Chapter 3)

3 cups shredded coconut

3-4 drops red food coloring (optional)

Makes 12 cakes
Prep Time: 20 minutes
Cook Time: 25 minutes
Finishing Time: 30 minutes

1. Preheat oven to 350°F. Coat a muffin tin with nonstick cooking spray, and insert paper cups. Beat shortening and sugar together until smooth, then set aside. Whip egg whites to stiff peaks and set aside. Combine evaporated milk and $1\frac{1}{2}$ teaspoons coconut extract. In a small bowl, sift together flour, baking powder, and salt and then add alternately to shortening mixture with milk. Lighten batter with $\frac{1}{3}$ of the egg whites, then fold in remaining whites until just combined.

2. Transfer batter to prepared muffin tins, filling $\frac{3}{4}$ full (be sure not to over-fill, because cakes will be served upside-down). Bake 25 minutes, until firm, and a pick inserted comes out clean. Cool completely.

3. Using a spoon, dig into the top center of the cake and hollow out the center, being careful to keep the removed cake in one piece.

4. Stir together Vanilla Frosting and remaining coconut extract, and spoon 1-2 tablespoons into the middle of each cake. Replace cake top, turn upside down, and frost bottom and sides, so that the cake resembles a dome.

5. Combine shredded coconut and food coloring, mixing to reach a uniform pink color. Roll cake dome into coconut until well covered.

Cream-Filled Sponge Cake

You will recognize this cake right away. It's the one that puts a *Twinkle* in your eye.

6 eggs

¾ cup sugar

1¾ cups cake flour

1 tsp. vanilla extract

1 cup Simple Syrup (see Chapter 3)

½ recipe Sweetened Whipped Cream (see Chapter 3)

½ recipe Vanilla Frosting (see Chapter 3)

Makes 6 mini cakes
Prep Time: 20 minutes
Cook Time: 20 minutes
Finishing Time: 30 minutes

1. Preheat the oven to 375°F. Coat six mini loaf pans with nonstick cooking spray.

2. Combine eggs and sugar in a large bowl. Set the bowl over a pot of simmering water and whisk continuously until eggs are warmed and sugar is dissolved. Remove from heat and continue whisking until thick, foamy, and pale yellow.

3. Sift flour and salt over eggs all at once and fold together, being careful not to deflate.

4. Transfer batter to prepared pans, filling ¾ full. Bake until golden brown and firm, about 15 to 20 minutes. Cool cakes 10 minutes, and while still warm, invert to remove from pans.

5. Brush each cake with Simple Syrup, then cool completely.

6. Fold together whipped cream and vanilla frosting. Use a chopstick to make a hole at each end of each cake.

7. Fit a pastry bag with a small plain pastry tip. Fill the bag with the cream mixture, insert the tip, and inject cream until you feel the cake expanding. Repeat on each end with all cakes.

Chapter 13

Rolled Cakes

In This Chapter

- ◆ Easy tricks for a perfect roll
- ◆ Mousse, cream, ganache, and jam fillings
- ◆ Dark chocolate, white chocolate, fruit, and nut rolls

In French, it is known as a *roulade*. We call it a jelly roll, even when there no jelly in sight. This ingenious style of cake is elegant and simple.

Roll Along

The beauty is in the rolling. This technique looks complicated, but therein lies its appeal. There is no special icing technique, no pastry bags, and no fancy piping.

The method begins with the cake. It must be thin and baked in a jelly roll pan—or any baking sheet with a lip. Spread the batter out evenly, and bake it until it just begins to color. If it bakes too long, the cake will be too firm, and it will crack instead of roll.

When the cake cools, loosen the edges, then invert the cake onto one large sheet (or several small sheets laid end to end) of plastic wrap covered with a light dusting of granulated sugar. The plastic wrap is the key to rolling, and the sugar is the secret to avoid sticking.

Some cakes require a light soaking of Simple Syrup (see Chapter 3) to keep them moist before the filling is added. This is generally true with sponge-style cakes that have little fat in the batter. This soak is an excellent time to add a bit of flavor if the mood strikes you. Extracts, liqueurs, or coffee mixed into the Simple Syrup can add an extra layer of flavor.

Next, spread the filling in a thin, even layer. Stop about one-half inch from all the edges to keep the filling from oozing out as you roll.

Position the rectangle so that a long edge is closest to you. Begin rolling from that edge by first folding a little of the edge inward. Then, grab the plastic wrap closest to you and lift it up and away from you. This will force the cake to roll. Hold the plastic wrap with two hands to promote even rolling. When your cake is rolled up and surrounded by the plastic wrap, twist the ends of the wrap to tighten your loaf (like a sausage), and refrigerate to set the filling into shape.

Pre-Rolling

Some cooks like to pre-roll their cake before the filling is added, while it is still hot. Certain cakes give a little more when hot. This step stretches out the crumb and keeps it from cracking when it is finally rolled with filling.

To do this, sprinkle the cake with sugar and sandwich it between two sheets of plastic wrap to keep it from sticking. Roll it up, hold it for 10 to 20 seconds, then unroll it and let it cool.

Unfortunately, this pre-rolling technique doesn't work with every cake. Those that have a lot of butter are more delicate and tender when hot and can fall apart. Reserve this technique for cakes with an egg foam (such as a sponge cake) because they are more resilient.

If you experience cracking as your cake rolls, don't despair. It's normal, and it is rarely noticed in the finished product.

Serving

Store-bought rolled cakes are generally eaten before anyone even considers presentation. But in case your intention is to serve your rolled cakes on plates, there are some interesting ways to cut them.

Slices, like spiral coins, can be cut from the end one-half to one inch thick. They can be fanned out on a serving platter or plated with three to four slices per person, a dollop of cream, and some fresh fruit.

Bias cuts make a stunning presentation as well. Sliced on an angle, the slant accentuates the spiral filling and draws attention to your handiwork.

Of course, you can also just lob off a hunk and eat it. Or wrap it in foil like your favorite store brand and tuck it into somebody's lunch box.

Chocolate-Filled Chocolate Roll

This is for the chocoholics in your midst.

4 cups cake flour

1 cup cocoa powder

1 TB. plus 1½ tsp. baking soda

½ tsp. kosher salt

6 eggs, divided

3 cups sugar, divided

1 cup canola oil

1½ cups buttermilk

1½ cups strong brewed coffee

½ cup Simple Syrup (see Chapter 3)

1 recipe Ganache, room temperature (see Chapter 3)

¼ cup powdered sugar

Serves 6 to 8
Prep Time: 20 minutes
Cook Time: 10 minutes
Finishing Time: 90 minutes

1. Preheat the oven to 350°F. Coat a baking sheet with nonstick cooking spray, line it with parchment paper, and coat the paper with nonstick cooking spray.

2. Sift together flour, cocoa powder, baking soda, and salt; set aside.

3. In a large bowl, whip together eggs and 2⅔ cups sugar until fluffy and pale yellow, about five minutes.

4. Combine oil, buttermilk, and coffee and add alternately to eggs with dry mixture.

5. Transfer to the prepared pan and bake until set but springy to the touch, about 10 minutes. Cool completely.

6. Lay out a sheet or two of plastic wrap onto the counter so that it forms an area two inches larger than the baking pan. Dust the plastic wrap with sugar, then invert cake into the center.

7. Remove the parchment paper from cake and brush entire surface lightly with Simple Syrup. Spread ganache in a smooth, even layer (no thicker than $1/4$ inch).

8. Working from a long edge, roll the cake into a log using the plastic to help. Tighten the ends of the plastic wrap to force the cake into a sausage shape, and chill for at least one hour.

Tidbits

The coffee in this recipe is not added to produce a mocha flavor but rather to accentuate the bitter quality of the chocolate.

9. Unwrap chilled cake and dust with powdered sugar before serving.

Chocolate-Covered Banana Roll

This roll is like a chocolate-covered banana—only cakier. Be sure to use bananas that are ripe but not too ripe. They should be a little firm to hold up to the rolling.

1/2 cup cake flour

1 1/2 cups almond meal

2 cups powdered sugar

1/2 tsp. kosher salt

7 egg whites

1 cup (2 sticks) unsalted butter, melted

6 bananas, divided

1 cup Simple Syrup (see Chapter 3)

1 recipe Ganache, room temperature (see Chapter 3)

2 cups almonds, chopped

Serves 6 to 8
Prep Time: 20 minutes
Cook Time: 10 minutes
Finishing Time: 90 minutes

1. Preheat the oven to 350°F. Coat a baking sheet with nonstick cooking spray, line it with parchment paper, and coat the paper with nonstick cooking spray.

2. In a large bowl, stir together flour, almond meal, powdered sugar, and salt. Add egg whites all at once and beat until smooth, about three minutes. Add melted butter and beat another three minutes.

3. Chop three bananas finely and fold them into batter.

4. Transfer to the prepared pan and bake until set but springy to the touch, about 10 minutes. Cool completely.

5. Lay out a sheet or two of plastic wrap onto the counter so that it forms an area two inches larger than the baking pan. Dust the plastic wrap with sugar, then invert cake into the center.

6. Remove the parchment paper from the cake, brush entire surface lightly with Simple Syrup, then spread ganache in a smooth, even layer (no thicker than 1/4 inch).

7. Peel remaining bananas and lay end to end along the long edge of the cake.

8. Roll the cake around bananas and up into a log, using the plastic to help. Tighten the ends of the plastic wrap to force cake into a sausage shape; chill for at least one hour.

9. Unwrap chilled cake, ice with a thin layer of ganache, and top with chopped almonds. Chill again briefly to set before serving.

Helpful Hints

The perfect banana should be yellow all over with no green and very little brown. For maximum control over the ripeness of your bananas, buy them green and let them ripen, undisturbed, on your counter.

Cream-Filled Chocolate Roll

These are simple, but ... *ho, ho, ho,* are they delicious.

¾ cup water

¾ cup semisweet chocolate chips

1 cup (2 sticks) unsalted butter

1 cup brown sugar

3 eggs

4¼ cups cake flour

1½ tsp. baking soda

½ tsp. baking powder

¼ tsp. kosher salt

⅔ cup sour cream

¼ cup Simple Syrup (see Chapter 3)

½ recipe Sweetened Whipped Cream (see Chapter 3)

½ recipe Ganache, room temperature (see Chapter 3)

Chocolate shavings to decorate

Serves 6 to 8
Prep Time: 20 minutes
Cook Time: 10 minutes
Finishing Time: 90 minutes

1. Preheat the oven to 350°F. Coat a baking sheet with nonstick cooking spray, line it with parchment paper, and coat the paper with nonstick cooking spray.

2. In a small saucepan, combine water and chocolate chips. Place over high heat and bring to a boil, stirring until melted. Remove from heat and cool.

3. In a large bowl, beat together butter and brown sugar until creamy and smooth. Add eggs one by one, then add cooled chocolate and combine thoroughly.

4. Sift together cake flour, baking soda, baking powder, and salt and add alternately with sour cream.

5. Transfer to the prepared pan and bake until set but springy to the touch, about 10 minutes. Cool completely.

6. Lay out a sheet or two of plastic wrap onto the counter so that it forms an area two inches larger than the baking pan. Dust the plastic wrap with sugar, then invert cake into the center.

7. Remove the parchment paper from cake, brush the entire surface lightly with Simple Syrup, then cover with a smooth, even layer of whipped cream no thicker than $^1/_4$ inch.

8. Working from a long edge, roll cake into a log using the plastic to help. Tighten the ends of the plastic wrap to force cake into a sausage shape; chill for at least one hour.

9. Unwrap chilled cake, frost with ganache, and chill again briefly to set. Top with chocolate shavings before serving.

 Heads Up

Whipped cream will continue to whip as you spread it. To avoid overwhipping at that stage, slightly underwhip it initially.

Jelly Rolls

This is the classic recipe. I prefer raspberry jam, but any jam will do.

½ cup (1 stick) unsalted butter

1 cup sugar

2 eggs

1½ cups buttermilk

1 TB. vanilla extract

1½ cups cake flour

1 TB. baking powder

½ tsp. kosher salt

2 cups raspberry jam

½ cup Simple Syrup (see Chapter 3)

¼ cup powdered sugar

Serves 6 to 8
Prep Time: 20 minutes
Cook Time: 10 minutes
Finishing Time: 90 minutes

1. Preheat the oven to 350°F. Coat a baking sheet with nonstick cooking spray, line it with parchment paper, and coat the paper with nonstick cooking spray.

2. Beat butter and sugar together until smooth. Add eggs one by one. Combine buttermilk and vanilla extract; set aside.

3. Sift together flour, baking powder, and salt and add alternately to buttermilk mixture. Transfer to prepared pan and bake until set but springy to the touch, about 10 minutes. Cool completely.

4. Lay out a sheet or two of plastic wrap onto the counter so that it forms an area two inches larger than the baking pan. Dust the plastic wrap with sugar, then invert cake into the center.

5. Remove the parchment paper from cake and brush the entire surface with Simple Syrup. Spread jam in a smooth, even layer (no thicker than ¼ inch).

6. Roll into a log using the plastic wrap to help. Tighten the ends of the plastic wrap to force cake into a sausage shape; chill for at least one hour. Unwrap chilled cake and dust with powdered sugar before serving.

Maple Walnut Roll

Maple isn't just for pancakes anymore. Its sweet, distinctive flavor is the perfect match for rich, toasted walnuts—whatever time it is.

¾ cup (1½ sticks) unsalted butter

1½ cups powdered sugar, sifted and divided

5 eggs, separated

3 cups walnuts, chopped finely

1 tsp. maple extract

1 tsp. lemon juice

¾ cup bread flour

½ cup sugar

1 recipe Vanilla Frosting (see Chapter 3), replacing cream with an equal amount of maple syrup

Serves 6 to 8
Prep Time: 20 minutes
Cook Time: 10 minutes
Finishing Time: 90 minutes

1. Preheat the oven to 350°F. Coat a baking sheet with nonstick cooking spray, line it with parchment paper, and coat the paper with nonstick cooking spray.

2. Beat together butter and ¾ cup powdered sugar until smooth and creamy. Add yolks one by one, then add vanilla and lemon juice. Set aside.

3. Whip egg whites to medium peaks. Slowly add remaining powdered sugar and continue whipping to stiff peaks. Sift flour over egg whites and fold together partially.

4. Add egg white mixture to creamed mixture and continue folding until well incorporated.

5. Transfer to the prepared pan and bake until set but springy to the touch, about 10 minutes. Cool completely.

6. Lay out a sheet or two of plastic wrap onto the counter so that it forms an area two inches larger than the baking pan. Dust the plastic wrap with sugar, then invert cake into the center.

7. Remove the parchment paper from cake and brush the entire surface lightly with Simple Syrup. Spread maple frosting in a smooth, even layer (no thicker than 1/4 inch).

8. Roll into a log, using the plastic wrap to help. Tighten the ends of the plastic wrap to force cake into a sausage shape; chill for at least one hour.

9. Unwrap chilled cake and top with remaining frosting and remaining walnuts. Chill again briefly to set before serving.

Tidbits

There is nothing like real maple syrup. Most of the syrup on your grocer's shelf is flavored corn syrup. The real thing comes from sugar or black maple trees. When the nights freeze and the days are warm, the sap begins to flow. It is collected and sent to the sugar house (or sugar shack) for sugaring off—a slow evaporation. The resulting syrup is thinner than the corn syrup stuff but much more flavorful.

Orange Marmalade Roulade

This refreshing citrus cake is perfect with a cup of tea.

½ cup (1 stick) unsalted butter

1 cup sugar

Zest and juice of three oranges, separated

2 eggs

2 cups cake flour

1 tsp. baking soda

½ tsp. kosher salt

⅔ cup sour cream

1 tsp. vanilla extract

1 cup Simple Syrup (see Chapter 3)

2 cups orange marmalade

1 recipe Sweetened Whipped Cream
(see Chapter 3)

¼ cup powdered sugar

Serves 6 to 8
Prep Time: 20 minutes
Cook Time: 10 minutes
Finishing Time: 90 minutes

1. Preheat the oven to 350°F. Coat a baking sheet with nonstick cooking spray, line it with parchment paper, and coat the paper with nonstick cooking spray.

2. Beat together butter, sugar, and orange zest until creamy and smooth. Add eggs one by one.

3. Sift together flour, baking soda, and salt and add alternately with sour cream. Stir in vanilla.

4. Transfer to the prepared pan and bake until set but springy to the touch, about 10 minutes. Cool completely.

5. Lay out a sheet or two of plastic wrap onto the counter so that it forms an area two inches larger than the baking pan. Dust the plastic wrap with sugar, then invert cake into the center. Remove the parchment paper from cake.

6. Combine orange juice and Simple Syrup; brush entire surface of cake lightly.

7. Fold marmalade into whipped cream, then spread onto cake in a smooth, even layer (no thicker than $^1/_4$ inch).

8. Roll into a log, using the plastic wrap to help. Tighten the ends of the plastic wrap to force cake into a sausage shape; chill for at least one hour.

9. Unwrap chilled cake and dust with powdered sugar before serving.

Tidbits

Today, marmalade refers to a jam made from citrus fruit. The rind, pith, and fruit are chopped together and cooked with sugar to produce a jam consistency. But the root of the word, *marmelo,* is derived from the Latin word for quince, a cousin of apples and pears. Indeed, the ancient Romans and Greeks had a sweet preserve made from the quince

White Chocolate Summer Fruit Roll

In this cake, the rich, buttery white chocolate is set off by the acidity of summer fruits. This cake is a perfect foundation for seasonal variations. Make the filling with cranberries, pears, and pomegranates in the fall, assorted citrus fruits in winter, and rhubarb in the spring.

1 cup white chocolate chips

¾ cup water

1 cup (2 sticks) butter

1 cup plus 2 TB. sugar

1 tsp. vanilla extract

3 eggs

3½ cups cake flour

1½ tsp. baking soda

½ tsp. baking powder

½ tsp. kosher salt

⅔ cup buttermilk

1 recipe Sweetened Whipped Cream
(see Chapter 3), chocolate cream variation,
made with white chocolate chips

1 pint raspberries

1 pint blackberries

1 cup diced peaches

1 cup diced kiwi fruit

¼ cup powdered sugar

Serves 6 to 8
Prep Time: 20 minutes
Cook Time: 10 minutes
Finishing Time: 90 minutes

1. Preheat the oven to 350°F. Coat a baking sheet with nonstick cooking spray, line it with parchment paper, and coat the paper with nonstick cooking spray.

2. Combine white chocolate and water in a small saucepan over medium heat. Heat gently, stirring until melted. Set aside.

3. Beat butter and sugar together until smooth and creamy. Add eggs one at a time, then add cooled white chocolate.

4. Sift together flour, baking soda, baking powder, and salt and add alternately with buttermilk.

5. Transfer to the prepared pan and bake until set but springy to the touch, about 10 minutes. Cool completely.

6. Lay out a sheet or two of plastic wrap onto the counter so that it forms an area two inches larger than the baking pan. Dust the plastic wrap with sugar, then invert cake into the center. Remove the parchment paper from cake.

7. Spread white chocolate whipped cream in a smooth, even layer (no thicker than $^1/4$ inch). Scatter fruit in a single, even layer across cream.

8. Roll into a log, using the plastic wrap to help. Tighten the ends of the plastic wrap to force cake into a sausage shape; chill for at least one hour. Unwrap chilled cake and dust with powdered sugar before serving.

Tidbits _____

White chocolate cannot technically be called chocolate because it contains no cocoa bean solids—or what is known in the chocolate industry as *chocolate liquor*. The white version is made from cocoa butter, vanilla, milk, and sugar.

Chapter 14

Sandwich Cakes

In This Chapter

- Sweet sandwich "bread" made with cookies, cakes, brownies, and bars
- Sweet sandwich fillings of frosting, cream, fruit jam, custard, and ice cream
- Round, square, and rectangular sandwiches

The beauty of the sandwich is that it can be made from anything. Creating them is never more fun than it is in the land of sweet snacks. Here, the "bread" can be cookies, cakes, brownies, or bars. The "meat" of the sandwich has even more possibilities. Frostings, jams, creams, custards, and even ice cream are all viable options. Sweet sandwiches can be iced and decorated, too, unlike their savory counterparts.

Keeping It Together

When creating a sweet sandwich, an important consideration is the stability of the "bread." Because these concoctions are generally eaten with your hands, the "bread" needs to be firm and sturdy.

Several of the recipes in this chapter are based on cookie dough while some originate as cakes. In both cases, attention should be paid to the mixing.

If butter is overcreamed, the batter will spread too much in the oven. If an egg foam is overfolded, the batter will be too thin.

Stuck in the Middle

The "meat" of a sweet sandwich also needs some attention. It, too, should be somewhat firm. If it's too gooey or runny, you and your friends will have trouble eating it.

Sandwiches filled with ice cream must be kept in the freezer. They need at least an hour after assembly to harden back up before they are served. If they're enjoyed too soon, the filling will ooze out with every bite.

Any filling that contains chocolate should chill for at least an hour before eating. Chocolate solidifies when refrigerated—and even when mixed with whipped cream, the chill will help stabilize the center and make eating easier. Butter-based fillings, too, like chocolate or vanilla frosting, benefit from chilling out.

Let's Celebrate!

After you read this chapter, you will no doubt come up with some sandwich ideas of your own. Test them on your friends and throw an ice cream sandwich party—perhaps on August 2nd, which is National Ice Cream Sandwich Day.

Chocolate-Chocolate Chip Sandwich

These ice cream cookie sandwiches can be tailored to order. Make cookies of varying sizes to fit the hands of various people. Mini cookies are turned into frozen bite-size treats, and giant cookies can be sliced like a cake into sandwich wedges.

2¾ cups all-purpose flour

1 tsp. baking soda

½ tsp. kosher salt

¾ cup (1½ sticks) unsalted butter

1 cup sugar

1 cup brown sugar

1 TB. vanilla extract

2 eggs

2 cups chocolate chips

1 qt. chocolate ice cream

1 recipe Chocolate Ganache, glaze variation (see Chapter 3)

> **Makes about 10 to 12 sandwiches**
>
> **Prep Time:** 20 minutes
>
> **Cook Time:** 15 minutes
>
> **Finishing Time:** 60 minutes

1. Preheat the oven to 325°F. Line two baking sheets with parchment paper.

2. Beat butter and sugars together until smooth and creamy. Add vanilla and eggs one by one.

3. Sift together flour, baking soda, and salt and slowly add to butter mixture. Mix well to fully incorporate; fold in chips.

4. Scoop batter by heaping tablespoons two inches apart onto prepared pans. Bake for 10 to 15 minutes until golden brown on the edges. Cool completely.

5. Sandwich a large, rounded scoop of chocolate ice cream between two cookies. Dip cookie tops into ganache, place on a parchment-lined baking sheet, and freeze at least one hour to set.

Helpful Hints

Make this dough ahead of time and keep it in the freezer for up to a week. Rolling it into logs makes cooking a snap. Simply slice off ¹/₂-inch coins and bake.

Devil's Food Ice Cream Sandwich

These sandwiches could be finished with a chocolate glaze, but they are more reminiscent of the quintessential, old-fashioned ice cream sandwich without it.

$\frac{1}{2}$ cup (1 stick) unsalted butter

$1\frac{1}{2}$ cups sugar

2 eggs

$\frac{1}{2}$ cup water

2 cups cake flour

$\frac{1}{2}$ cup cocoa

$\frac{1}{2}$ tsp. baking soda

$\frac{1}{2}$ tsp. kosher salt

$\frac{1}{2}$ cup milk

1 tsp. vanilla extract

1 qt. vanilla ice cream

$\frac{1}{4}$ cup powdered sugar

Makes about 6 to 8 sandwiches

Prep Time: 20 minutes

Cook Time: 5 minutes

Finishing Time: 10 minutes

1. Preheat the oven to 350°F. Coat two baking sheets with nonstick cooking spray, line them with parchment paper, and coat the paper with nonstick cooking spray.

2. In a large bowl, beat together butter and sugar until creamy and smooth. Add eggs one by one, then add water and beat until smooth.

3. Sift together flour, cocoa powder, baking soda, and salt and add alternately with milk. Stir in vanilla.

4. Divide batter between the two prepared pans, spreading very thinly. Bake until firm, about five minutes.

5. While still a little warm, cut cooled cake into 2×4-inch rectangles and let cool completely.

6. Use an ice cream spade to scoop a rectangular hunk of ice cream and sandwich it between two pieces of cake. Repeat with remaining cake, then place on the parchment-lined sheet and freeze at least one hour to set. Dust with powdered sugar before serving.

Heads Up

This cake is spread extra thinly to create the old-fashioned cake layers of an ice cream sandwich. Extra thin means extra easy to burn, so watch closely and rotate the pans every few minutes for even cooking.

Cream-Filled Chocolate Cake Sandwich

These sandwiches are simple but surprisingly elegant. This is a cake batter baked like a cookie. To make them uniform, use an ice cream scoop.

$^1\!/_2$ cup chocolate chips

$^1\!/_2$ cup water

1 cup (2 sticks) unsalted butter

2 cups sugar

4 eggs, separated

1 tsp. vanilla extract

2 cups all-purpose flour

1$^1\!/_2$ tsp. baking soda

$^1\!/_2$ tsp. kosher salt

1 cup buttermilk

1 recipe Sweetened Whipped Cream (see Chapter 3)

$^1\!/_4$ cup powdered sugar

Makes about 8 to 10 sandwiches

Prep Time: 20 minutes

Cook Time: 10 minutes

Finishing Time: 10 minutes

1. Preheat the oven to 350°F. Coat a baking sheet with nonstick cooking spray, line it with parchment paper, and coat the paper with nonstick cooking spray.

2. Combine chocolate and water in a small saucepan. Melt together, stirring over medium heat. Set aside to cool.

3. Beat butter and sugar together until smooth and creamy. Add egg yolks one by one, then add vanilla. Sift flour, baking soda, and salt and add alternately with buttermilk.

4. Whip egg whites to stiff peaks and fold gently into batter.

5. Drop by heaping tablespoons two inches apart onto the prepared pan. Bake until set, about 10 minutes. Cool completely.

6. Sandwich a dollop of cream between two cakes, dust with powdered sugar, and serve immediately. Cakes can be made ahead and sandwiched with cream at the last minute.

Chocolate-Covered Ice Cream Sandwich

What could be better than brownies and ice cream? Brownies and ice cream doused in chocolate, that's what!

1 cup (2 sticks) unsalted butter

1 cup chocolate chips

1½ cup sugar

4 eggs

1 tsp. vanilla extract

1 tsp. baking soda

1 tsp. kosher salt

1 cup all-purpose flour

1 quart vanilla ice cream

1 recipe Chocolate Ganache, glaze variation (Chapter 3)

> **Makes about 8 to 10 sandwiches**
>
> **Prep Time:** 20 minutes
>
> **Cook Time:** 25 minutes
>
> **Finishing Time:** 90 minutes

1. Preheat the oven to 325°F. Coat a baking sheet with nonstick cooking spray, line it with parchment paper, and coat the paper with nonstick cooking spray.

2. Melt butter and chocolate together over low heat, stirring until completely melted. Remove from heat and beat in sugar, eggs, and vanilla.

3. Sift together baking soda, salt, and flour, and beat into batter.

4. Transfer to prepared pan, spread smooth, and bake 20–25 minutes, until firm. Cool completely. Cut cooled brownies into 2×4 inch rectangles.

5. Use an ice cream spade to scoop a rectangular hunk of ice cream, and sandwich it between two brownies. Repeat with remaining brownies, then place on parchment-lined sheet and freeze at least one hour to set.

6. Dip frozen sandwiches into ganache glaze, and return to the freezer for 10 minutes to set.

Vanilla Ice Cream Oatmeal Cookie Sandwich

In the San Francisco Bay Area you can find these treats in every grocer's freezer section. *It's* definitely *It!*

¾ cup (1½ sticks) unsalted butter

1 cup sugar

1 cup brown sugar

2 eggs

1 TB. vanilla extract

1½ cups all-purpose flour

1 tsp. baking soda

½ tsp. kosher salt

2 cups rolled oats

1 recipe Ganache, glaze variation (Chapter 3)

> **Makes about 12 sandwiches**
>
> **Prep Time:** 20 minutes
> **Cook Time:** 10 minutes
> **Finishing Time:** 90 minutes

1. Preheat the oven to 350°F. Line two baking sheets with parchment paper.

2. Beat together butter, sugar, and brown sugar until smooth and creamy. Add eggs one by one, then add extract.

3. Sift together flour, baking soda, salt, and add. Stir in oats and mix well to fully incorporate.

4. Chill dough for 30 minutes.

5. Drop by heaping tablespoonful onto prepared pan, 2 inches apart. Bake until set, about 10 minutes. Cool completely.

6. Sandwich a large, rounded scoop of vanilla ice cream between two cookies. Repeat with remaining cookies, place on parchment-lined sheet, and freeze at least one hour to set.

7. Prepare ganache glaze, and dip each frozen sandwiches. Return to the freezer for 10 minutes to set.

Cream-Filled Oatmeal Sandwich

This recipe is an homage to one of the first mass-produced snack cakes. It is practically snack cake royalty. All hail Queen Debbie!

1 cup raisins

¾ cup boiling water

½ cup (1 stick) unsalted butter

½ cup brown sugar

1 egg

1 TB. vanilla

1 cup rolled oats

1½ cups all-purpose flour

1 tsp. cinnamon

1 tsp. nutmeg

1 tsp. ginger

¾ tsp. baking soda

½ tsp. kosher salt

1 recipe Sweetened Whipped Cream (Chapter 3)

½ recipe White Frosting (Chapter 3)

> **Makes about 8 to 10 sandwiches**
>
> **Prep Time:** 20 minutes
>
> **Cook Time:** 10 minutes
>
> **Finishing Time:** 10 minutes

1. Preheat the oven to 350°F. Coat a baking sheet with nonstick cooking spray, line it with parchment paper, and coat the paper with nonstick cooking spray.

2. Combine raisins and hot water, and set aside to plump for 30 minutes.

3. In a large bowl, beat together butter and brown sugar until smooth and creamy. Stir in egg, vanilla, then add oats.

4. Sift together flour, cinnamon, nutmeg, ginger, baking soda, and salt. Add alternately with raisins and water, and mix until well blended.

5. Drop by heaping tablespoonful onto prepared pan, 2 inches apart. Bake until set, about 10 minutes. Cool completely.

6. Fold whipped cream and frosting together, sandwich a generous dollop between two oatmeal cakes, and serve immediately. Cakes can be made ahead and sandwiched with cream at the last minute.

Heads Up

Both classic and quick rolled oats work in this recipe, but the fancier, heartier, steel-cut oats should be avoided. They won't soften enough in this batter, and the result is practically inedible.

Marshmallow-Filled Chocolate Sandwich

If I lived in the *Moon*, I'd want a *Pie* like this.

¾ cup (1½ sticks) unsalted butter

2 cups sugar

2 eggs

2 tsp. vanilla

2 cups all-purpose flour

¾ cup cocoa powder

1 tsp. baking soda

½ tsp. kosher salt

2-3 cups marshmallow cream

1 recipe Ganache, glaze variation (Chapter 3)

> **Makes about 8 to 10 sandwiches**
>
> **Prep Time:** 20 minutes
>
> **Cook Time:** 10 minutes
>
> **Finishing Time:** 10 minutes

1. Preheat the oven to 350°F. Coat a baking sheet with nonstick cooking spray, line it with parchment paper, and coat the paper with nonstick cooking spray.

2. In a large bowl, beat together butter and sugar until smooth and creamy. Stir in eggs, one by one, then vanilla.

3. Sift together flour, cocoa powder, baking soda, and salt, then add slowly and beat until well combined.

4. Drop by heaping tablespoonful onto prepared pan, 2 inches apart. Bake until set, about 10 minutes. Cool completely.

5. Sandwich a generous dollop of marshmallow creme between two chocolate cakes. Repeat with remaining cake, place on parchment-lined sheet and freeze at least one hour to set.

6. Prepare ganache glaze, dip each frozen sandwich, and return to the freezer for 10 minutes to set.

 Heads Up

Marshmallow creme (or fluff) is a food in constant motion. Don't let these sandwiches sit too long before serving, as the filling will ooze.

Peanut Butter and Jelly Sandwich Bars

If you're not a fan of grape jam, use whatever you like. Or omit the jam altogether and sandwich your peanut butter cookies with chocolate ganache, sliced bananas, marshmallow cream, or all three!

1¼ cups all-purpose flour

½ tsp. baking powder

½ tsp. kosher salt

½ cup (1 stick) butter

½ cup peanut butter (smooth or chunky)

1½ cups sugar, divided

½ cup brown sugar

1 TB. vanilla extract

1 egg

½ recipe Chocolate Ganache, glaze variation (Chapter 3)

½ cups concord grape jam

> **Makes about 12 sandwiches**
>
> **Prep Time:** 40 minutes
>
> **Cook Time:** 15 minutes
>
> **Finishing Time:** 30 minutes

1. Preheat the oven to 325°F. Line two baking sheets with parchment paper.

2. Beat together butter, peanut butter, ½ cup sugar, and brown sugar until smooth and creamy. Add vanilla and egg.

3. Sift together flour, baking soda, and salt, and add slowly. Mix well to fully incorporate, then chill dough for 30 minutes.

4. Fill a small bowl with the remaining granulated sugar. Roll cookie dough into walnut-size balls, coat them with sugar, and set onto lined baking sheets 2 inches apart.

5. Use a fork dipped in sugar to make a cross-hatch design. Bake at 325°F for 10-12 minutes, until golden brown on the edges. Cool completely.

6. Dip the flat side of each cookie into ganache, place on a parchment lined baking sheet, and chill until set. Sandwich a generous dollop of jam between two cookies, and serve.

Chapter 15

Mini Crumb Cakes

In This Chapter

◆ Cakes with nuts and chocolate

◆ Cakes with fruit and cream

◆ Cakes with flowers and berries

Crumb cakes can come from any category of cake, but they are usually considered a breakfast item.

Crumbs

The title "crumb" refers to a crisp, crumbly topping—generally some variation of streusel.

Streusel, from the German word *streusen* (meaning "to scatter"), has long been a popular cake topping in Europe but didn't gain popularity in the United States until World War II—probably because the crumb topping was quicker and easier to make than pie dough.

The streusel, a cut-in mixture of flour, sugar, and butter (see Chapter 3), can be embellished in a number of ways. Spices, nuts, oats, and a variety of sugars and flours can be used to give it a unique flavor.

Beyond this definition, crumb cakes vary widely.

Cakes

The cake found underneath the crumb is most frequently a butter cake or a batter based on the creaming together of butter and sugar. This method appears throughout this book, but it is worth taking a minute to review a couple of basic principles.

Batters can be mixed by hand or by machine. Take care not to overmix if a machine is used, however. If you're working by hand, be sure all the lumps are beaten out of the butter and sugar before you add eggs. Once the eggs go in, the lumps are permanent.

When the eggs and flavoring are added, the mixture may look broken—like cottage cheese. Relax! This is normal. As soon as the flour is added, the batter will come together nicely.

Pans

Crumb cakes in this chapter are baked in muffin tins. They can be made in any shape of mini pan, however. See Appendix B for a list of cookware resources. They also can be made in a large pan and served by the slice.

Baking this cake in a larger pan is simple. First, coat the pan with non-stick cooking spray and line the bottom with a circle of parchment cut to fit, then spray the circle. Fill the pan three quarters full with batter, then top it according to the recipe. Bake your cake at a lower temperature than directed for the small versions. A 20° to 25°F reduction is adequate to ensure that the outer crust will not burn while the center sets.

Cherry Crisp Crumb Cake

If it's cherry season, find the sweetest cherries you can. If it's not cherry season, feel free to use frozen cherries or even cherry pie filling for this recipe.

1 cup (2 sticks) unsalted butter

1 cup sugar

2 eggs

2 tsp. vanilla

3½ cups cake flour

1 tsp. baking powder

1 tsp. kosher salt

1 cup buttermilk

1½ cups fresh or frozen cherries, pitted

1 recipe Streusel (see Chapter 3)

> **Makes about 12 crumb cakes**
>
> **Prep Time:** 20 minutes
> **Cook Time:** 20 minutes

1. Preheat the oven to 375°F. Coat a muffin pan with nonstick cooking spray; line with paper cups.

2. Beat together butter and sugar until smooth and creamy. Add eggs one by one, then add vanilla.

3. Sift together cake flour, baking powder, and salt and add alternately with buttermilk.

4. Fill muffin tins ¾ full with batter. Top with cherries divided evenly between tins, then add streusel.

5. Bake until risen and firm to the touch, about 15 to 20 minutes. Cool 10 minutes, then remove from the pan.

Helpful Hints

When pitting cherries, it's a good idea to wear rubber gloves. The juice stains your skin and takes several days to wear off. An apron isn't a bad idea, either. While I prefer to simply break the cherries in half to remove the pit, some cooks like to use cherry-pitting gadgets.

Apple Brown Betty Cake

Most apples in the United States are grown and sold for lunch boxes, and all bake up pretty much the same. I always advise using the apple you prefer to eat out of hand. My favorite? The Fuji!

1 cup (2 sticks) unsalted butter, divided

4 large apples, peeled and diced

$\frac{1}{2}$ cup brown sugar

4 cups dry, plain bread crumbs

2 cups cake flour

1 cup sugar

1 tsp. ground nutmeg

1 TB. baking powder

$\frac{1}{2}$ tsp. kosher salt

4 egg yolks

$\frac{2}{3}$ cup buttermilk

Zest of 1 lemon

Makes about 12 crumb cakes

Prep Time: 40 minutes

Cook Time: 20 minutes

1. Melt $\frac{1}{4}$ cup ($\frac{1}{2}$ stick) butter in a large sauté pan over medium heat. Add apples and brown sugar; cook, stirring until apples are caramelized and tender, about 10 minutes.

2. Remove apples from pan; add another $\frac{1}{4}$ cup butter and melt. Add bread crumbs and cinnamon to melted butter and cook over high heat, stirring until toasted. Remove from heat and set aside.

3. Preheat the oven to 375°F. Coat a muffin tin with nonstick cooking spray and line it with paper cups.

4. In a large bowl, sift together flour, sugar, nutmeg, baking powder, and salt. Cut in $\frac{1}{2}$ cup (1 stick) butter until mixture resembles cornmeal.

5. Combine egg yolks, buttermilk, and lemon zest and beat into dry mixture until smooth.

6. Fill muffin tins $\frac{3}{4}$ full with batter. Top with apples, divided evenly between tins, then bread crumbs. Bake until risen and firm to the touch, about 15 to 20 minutes. Cool 10 minutes, then remove from the pan.

Orange Marble Crumb Cake

Orange and white, this marbled batter is all the same flavor with a little added color for appearance. You can omit the color if you like and go *au naturel*.

1 cup (2 sticks) unsalted butter

1 cup sugar

Zest and juice of 1 orange

2 eggs

1 tsp. orange extract

2 cups cake flour

1 tsp. baking soda

½ tsp. baking powder

½ tsp. kosher salt

1 cup sour cream

3 to 4 drops orange food color

1 (11-oz.) can mandarin oranges, drained

1 recipe Streusel (see Chapter 3)

> **Makes about 12 crumb cakes**
>
> **Prep Time:** 20 minutes
> **Cook Time:** 20 minutes

1. Preheat the oven to 375°F. Coat a muffin pan with nonstick cooking spray, then line with paper cups.

2. Beat together butter, sugar, and orange zest until smooth and creamy. Add eggs one by one, then add orange extract.

3. Sift together cake flour, baking soda, baking powder, and salt; add alternately with sour cream.

4. Fill muffin tins ⅓ full with batter. Add orange food color to remaining batter and use it to fill the tins ⅔ full. Fold batter in each cup briefly with a spoon.

5. Top with oranges divided evenly between tins, then top with streusel.

6. Bake until risen and firm to the touch, about 15 to 20 minutes. Cool 10 minutes, then remove from the pan.

Pumpkin Cream Cheese Crumb Cake

Canned pumpkin is always available, but if you'd like to make it from scratch, cut a pumpkin in half, scoop out the seeds, and roast it cut side down in a 450°F oven until soft, about 30 minutes. Then scoop out the pumpkin and puree or mash it until smooth. The following recipe makes a good Halloween treat or Thanksgiving dessert.

1 cup (2 sticks) unsalted butter

1½ cups brown sugar

4 large eggs

3 cups all-purpose flour

2 tsp. baking powder

1 tsp. ground cinnamon

1 tsp. ground nutmeg

½ tsp. ground ginger

¼ tsp. ground cloves

½ tsp. kosher salt

1 cup solid-pack pumpkin

½ cup milk

1 (8-oz.) pkg. cream cheese

⅓ cup sugar

1 recipe Streusel (see Chapter 3)

> **Makes about 12 crumb cakes**
>
> **Prep Time:** 20 minutes
>
> **Cook Time:** 20 minutes

1. Preheat the oven to 375°F. Coat a muffin pan with nonstick cooking spray, then line with paper cups.

2. Beat butter and sugar together until smooth and creamy. Add eggs one at a time.

3. Combine flour, baking powder, cinnamon, nutmeg, ginger, cloves, and salt. Set aside. Stir together pumpkin and milk and add to creamed mixture alternately with flour mixture. Fill the tins ¾ full with batter.

4. In a small bowl, beat cream cheese and sugar until smooth. Place a dollop in each tin and top with streusel. Bake until risen and firm to the touch, about 20 minutes. Cool 10 minutes before removing from the pan.

Helpful Hints

If you need to feed a crowd, this cake makes a stunning presentation when baked in an angel food cake pan. Reduce the oven temperature to 350°F and check for doneness by inserting a pick into the center of the cake, which should come out clean.

Toasted Almond Crumb Cake

The intense almond flavor of this cake can hold its own, even without the almond crumb topping. Try baking this batter in a loaf pan and serving slices with fresh peaches or apricots.

1 cup (2 sticks) unsalted butter

8 oz. almond paste

1 cups sugar

3 eggs

1 tsp. vanilla extract

1 tsp. almond extract

1 cup all-purpose flour

1 cup cake flour

1¼ tsp. baking powder

¾ tsp. kosher salt

¼ cup sour cream

1 cup sliced almonds

1 recipe Streusel (see Chapter 3)

Makes about 12 crumb cakes

Prep Time: 20 minutes

Cook Time: 20 minutes

1. Preheat the oven to 375°F. Coat a muffin pan with nonstick cooking spray, then line with paper cups.

2. Beat butter, almond paste, and sugar together until smooth and creamy. Add eggs one at a time, then add vanilla and almond extracts.

3. Combine flour, baking powder, and salt and add alternately with sour cream.

Tidbits

Almonds are related to the stone fruits: peaches, nectarines, and apricots. You can see the resemblance when you examine the pits of these fruits.

4. Fill tins ¾ full with batter. Mix streusel and almonds and top each crumb cake.

5. Bake until risen and firm, about 15 to 20 minutes. Cool 10 minutes before removing from the pan.

Victorian Rose Crumb Cake

The floral essence of this cake is subtle but heavenly. You can find rose-water and tiny edible rosebuds in Indian and Middle Eastern markets. Rosebuds are also commonly found in Latino markets.

1 cup (2 sticks) unsalted butter

1 cup sugar

4 eggs

1 TB. rosewater

2¼ cups cake flour

1 tsp. baking powder

¼ tsp. kosher salt

2 TB. milk

¼ cup dried rosebuds

1 recipe Streusel (Chapter 3)

> **Makes about 12 crumb cakes**
>
> **Prep Time:** 20 minutes
>
> **Cook Time:** 20 minutes

1. Preheat the oven to 375°F. Coat a muffin pan with nonstick cooking spray, then line with paper cups.

2. Beat butter and sugar together until smooth and creamy. Add eggs one at a time, then add rosewater.

3. Combine flour, baking powder, and salt and add alternately with milk. In a separate bowl, mix rosebuds and streusel.

4. Fill tins ¾ full with batter and top with streusel.

5. Bake until risen and firm, about 15 to 20 minutes. Cool 10 minutes before removing from the pan.

Tidbits

Rosewater, brought back to Europe from colonial India, became a popular flavoring during the Victorian era—so much so that homemakers in America began distilling their own.

Tropical Crumb Cake

¾ cup (1½ sticks) butter

1½ cups brown sugar

3 eggs

1 TB. vanilla

3 cups cake flour

1½ tsp. baking soda

1 tsp. kosher salt

2 tsp. cinnamon

1 cup sour cream

1 cup shredded coconut

½ cup toasted macadamia nuts, chopped

1 recipe Streusel (see Chapter 3)

1 cup mango, diced

1 cup pineapple, diced

> **Makes about
> 12 crumb cakes**
>
> **Prep Time:** 20 minutes
> **Cook Time:** 20 minutes

1. Preheat the oven to 375°F. Coat a muffin pan with nonstick cooking spray, then line with paper cups.

2. Beat butter and brown sugar together until smooth and creamy. Add eggs one at a time, then add vanilla.

3. Combine flour, baking soda, salt, and cinnamon and add alternately with sour cream. In a separate bowl, mix coconut, macadamia nuts, and streusel.

4. Fill tins ⅓ full with batter. Add a tablespoon of streusel mix to each cup, then top with more batter to ⅔ full. Top with mango and pineapple divided evenly between each tin, and finish with a topping of streusel mix.

5. Bake until risen and firm, about 15 to 20 minutes. Cool 10 minutes before removing from the pan.

Chapter 16

Mini Fruitcakes

In This Chapter

- ◆ Classic holiday fruitcakes
- ◆ Tropical fruitcakes
- ◆ Spicy, nutty fruitcakes

Why does fruitcake get such a bad reputation? And why do we use it as a term denoting craziness? It should be a term that indicates deliciousness!

I blame the mass-produced, mail-order cakes laden with red and green candied cherries. They have little fruit and even less cake. Real fruitcake made with loving hands (not machinery) is a wonderful way to express your affection.

A Regal History

Sweet cakes and yeast breads can be found throughout history. Early Roman recipes show cakes of grains mixed with nuts and pomegranates. Medieval chefs created cakes with honey, fruit, and spices.

Such creations have been popular in Europe for centuries, especially during the holidays. This is because dried fruits, nuts, and honey were traditionally luxurious ingredients reserved for special occasions. In Britain, they eat a Christmas, or figgy, pudding. Unlike the custard-type pudding, these figgy puddings are cakes that are steamed, not baked. They are made with nuts, apples, dried fruits, spices, and some type of alcohol (which preserves the cake, often for up to a year).

In Russia, the *kulich* is a traditional yeast Easter bread with dried fruits, nuts, and a dough flavored with saffron. It is typically served with *pashka*, a fresh molded cheese made with honey, fruits, nuts, and spices.

The German version of fruitcake is the *stollen*, a yeast bread filled with candied citrus and dried fruits and flavored with cardamom. It is not a sweet dough, but the outside is heavily coated with powdered sugar. The shape of the loaf is meant to represent the baby Jesus in swaddling clothes.

In Mexico, the *rosca de reyes*, or king's bread, is a similar yeast bread found at Christmastime. Shaped in a ring, it is filled with fruit and covered with sweet white icing.

Fruits

Any fruit can be used in a fruitcake, but generally dried fruits are found in holiday cakes. That is because the dried fruits were traditionally the only fruits available in the winter. Raisins, figs, and dates are the most common as well as candied citrus peel.

Candied peel can be bought in specialty food stores or on the Internet, but it is simple to make yourself. Peel oranges and lemons and dice the peel into quarter-inch cubes. Blanch first in boiling water to remove the bitterness, then simmer in Simple Syrup (see Chapter 3) for two to three hours until tender and sweet. Drain and store, submerged in sugar, in an airtight container or freeze in plastic zipper bags.

Ambrosia Cake

Ambrosia is the food of the gods. It's also a salad made with gelatin and loaded with fruit and marshmallows. This cake takes the flavors of that salad and combines them in a snack cake fit for the gods.

2 cups all-purpose flour

1 TB. baking powder

½ tsp. kosher salt

½ cup (1 stick) unsalted butter

1 cup sugar

4 egg whites

1 TB. vanilla extract

½ cup milk

1 cup shredded coconut

1 (11-oz.) can mandarin oranges, drained

1 cup (about one 12-oz. jar, drained) maraschino cherries, halved

1 cup mini marshmallows

Makes 12 mini cakes
Prep Time: 20 minutes
Cook Time: 25 minutes
Finishing Time: 30 minutes

1. Preheat the oven to 350°F. Coat a muffin tin with nonstick cooking spray, then insert paper cups.

2. Beat butter and sugar together until smooth; set aside.

3. Whip egg whites to stiff peaks; set aside.

4. Combine milk and coconut extract; set aside.

5. Sift together flour, baking powder, and salt and add alternately to shortening mixture with milk.

6. Fold in coconut, oranges, cherries, and marshmallows. Lighten batter with ⅓ egg whites, then fold in remaining whites until just combined.

7. Transfer batter to prepared muffin tins, filling to the rim. Bake 25 minutes until firm and a pick inserted in the center comes out clean. Cool completely.

Applesauce Cake

Applesauce adds sweet moisture to this butter cake. Brown sugar and apple pie spices give it apple pie appeal.

½ cup (1 stick) unsalted butter

1 cup brown sugar

Zest of 1 lemon

1 egg

2 cups cake flour

1 tsp. baking soda

¼ tsp. kosher salt

1 tsp. ground cinnamon

1 tsp. ground nutmeg

¼ tsp. ground cloves

1 cup applesauce

1 cup raisins

Serves 6
Prep Time: 20 minutes
Cook Time: 20 minutes

1. Preheat the oven to 375°F. Coat six mini bundt pans with nonstick cooking spray.

2. Beat butter, sugar, and lemon zest together until smooth and creamy.

3. Sift together flour, baking soda, salt, cinnamon, nutmeg, and cloves and add alternately with applesauce. Fold in raisins.

4. Fill prepared tins ¾ full and bake until risen and firm, about 15 to 20 minutes. Cool 10 minutes before removing from pan.

Helpful Hints

This cake works especially well as a large cake. Lower the oven temperature to 350°F and give it 45 to 50 minutes in the oven. Sliced and toasted, it cries out for a slathering of cream cheese.

Cherry Upside-Down Cake

Upside-down cakes can be made individually, but nothing makes a grander statement than a large cake with hidden nuggets of fruit. Review Chapter 2 for information about switching pan sizes.

½ cup brown sugar, packed

1½ cups pitted cherries

3 cups cake flour

1½ tsp. baking soda

1 tsp. salt

2 tsp. cinnamon

12 oz. (1½ sticks) butter

1½ cups brown sugar

3 eggs

1 TB. vanilla

1 cup sour cream

1 recipe Streusel

Serves 10 to 12
Prep Time: 20 minutes
Cook Time: 30-45 minutes

1. Preheat oven to 350°F. Coat a 10-inch round baking pan with pan spray, and line with a circle of parchment paper. Sprinkle brown sugar evenly across bottom of pan, top with cherries, and set aside.

2. Sift together flour, baking soda, salt, cinnamon, and set aside. In a large bowl, beat together butter and brown sugar until creamy. Add eggs one at a time, mixing until smooth. Add sifted dry ingredients alternately with the sour cream, and mix until well blended.

3. Pour batter into the pan on top of cherries. Bake at 350°F for 30-45 minutes, until golden brown and a pick inserted into the center of the cake comes out clean. Cool 5 minutes, then invert onto serving platter.

 Helpful Hints

Cherries are a seasonal fruit, but can be found year-round in cans, or in the freezer section. If you have canned cherries, be sure to drain away all the juices before using them in this recipe.

Christmas Fruitcake

These cakes age well. Make them a week ahead and wrap them airtight. Then, before serving (or gifting), drizzle with icing.

$\frac{1}{2}$ cup golden raisins

$\frac{1}{2}$ cup currants

$\frac{1}{2}$ cup candied orange peel

$\frac{1}{2}$ cup candied lemon peel

$\frac{1}{4}$ cup maraschino cherries, chopped

$\frac{1}{4}$ cup candied *angelica*, chopped

1 cup brandy

1 cup (2 sticks) unsalted butter

1 cup sugar

5 eggs, separated

1 tsp. lemon juice

$2\frac{1}{4}$ cups all-purpose flour

2 tsp. ground nutmeg, divided

$\frac{1}{2}$ tsp. kosher salt

1 recipe White Glaze (see Chapter 3)

Serves 6
Prep Time: 30 minutes, plus overnight fruit soak
Cook Time: 25 minutes

1. Stir together raisins, currants, orange peel, lemon peel, cherries, angelica, and brandy. Let stand at room temperature overnight.

2. Preheat the oven to 350°F. Coat six mini bundt pans with nonstick cooking spray.

3. In a large bowl, beat together butter and sugar until smooth and creamy. Add egg yolks one by one and mix thoroughly.

4. Sift together flour, one teaspoon nutmeg, and salt; add alternately with fruit.

5. Whip egg whites to stiff peaks. Lighten batter with $\frac{1}{3}$ whites, then gently fold in remaining whites.

6. Fill prepared pans ¾ full of batter and bake until risen and firm, about 20 to 25 minutes. Cool cakes 10 minutes before removing from the pans.

7. Stir together White Glaze and remaining nutmeg. Drizzle over cooled cakes and serve.

Sweet Talk

Angelica is a giant herb in the parsley family. The stalks have a subtle licorice, anise, and sage flavor and are eaten as a vegetable in Scandinavian cuisines. The seeds are among the many herbs used to flavor vermouth, Chartreuse, and gin. The sweet root is used in jellies, fruit sauces, and potpourri. But by far, the most common application of angelica is the candied stem. Bright green, it is folded into fruitcakes around the world.

Panettone

This Italian sweet yeast bread is filled with dried fruits, nuts, and citrus peel. It is a traditional holiday bread, but why wait until then? It makes terrific French toast.

¼ cup golden raisins

¼ cup dark raisins

¼ cup candied orange peel

¼ cup candied lemon peel

Zest of 1 orange

Zest of 1 lemon

1 cup rum

¾ cup warm water

1 (.25-oz.) pkg. active dry yeast

¼ cup sugar

1 eggs

1 TB. vanilla extract

4 TB (½ stick) unsalted butter, softened

½ tsp. kosher salt

2-4 cups bread flour

½ cup milk

1 cup powdered sugar

Serves 6 to 8
Prep Time: 2 hours
Cook Time: 90 minutes

1. Stir together raisins, orange peel, lemon peel, orange zest, lemon zest, and rum; set at room temperature overnight.

2. In a medium bowl, combine warm water, yeast, and sugar and mix well to combine.

3. Add eggs, butter, salt, and fruit; mix thoroughly.

4. Add half the flour and stir to combine. Continue adding flour to create a firm dough.

5. Turn the dough onto a floured surface and knead, adding flour only when necessary until the dough becomes smooth and elastic (about 8 to 10 minutes).

6. Return dough to the bowl, cover with plastic wrap, and set in a warm place to rise until doubled in volume (about one hour).

7. Coat muffin pans with nonstick cooking spray, then line with paper cups.

8. Turn dough onto a floured surface and roll into a snake shape. Cut into two- to three-inch sections, roll into tight balls, and place into prepared tins.

9. Dust lightly with flour, cover with plastic wrap, and set aside to rise again for 30 minutes.

10. Preheat oven to 350°F.

11. Brush with milk and bake 20 to 30 minutes until risen and golden brown. Cool 10 minutes, remove from tins, and cool completely. Dust with powdered sugar.

Tidbits

This bread is associated with Milan and is traditionally baked in a cylindrical-shaped, or cupola, mold. Muffin tins are close, but you can make a more authentic shape by using clean soup cans or larger coffee cans. Clean them out and use a can opener to poke two to three holes in the bottom. This releases vacuum pressure that builds up in the heat of the oven. Spray the cans well with nonstick cooking spray, and line the sides with a cylinder of parchment.

Pineapple Upside-Down Cake

This classic cake is always a crowd pleaser. These mini muffin-size versions are cute when inverted to show off the gooey brown sugar–coated fruit.

½ cup brown sugar, packed

1 cup maraschino cherries, halved

1 (11-oz.) can crushed pineapple

½ cup (1 stick) unsalted butter

1 cup sugar

1 egg

½ tsp. vanilla extract

1¾ cups all-purpose flour

1 tsp. baking soda

½ tsp. kosher salt

1 cup milk

Makes 12 mini cakes

Prep Time: 20 minutes

Cook Time: 40 minutes

1. Preheat the oven to 350°F. Coat a muffin pan with nonstick cooking spray.

2. Divide brown sugar evenly between each tin. Place a half cherry in the center of each tin, then top with one tablespoon pineapple. Set aside.

3. Beat butter and sugar until smooth and creamy. Add egg and vanilla.

4. In a separate bowl, sift together flour, baking soda, and salt and add alternately with milk.

5. Pour batter over pineapple and bake 15 to 20 minutes until risen and firm.

6. Cool five minutes, then invert onto a serving platter.

Heads Up

While muffin tins usually get lined with paper cups, in this applica- tion it's a bad idea. There is so much juice and gooey caramel that the paper gets too wet and won't hold together. Therefore, be sure to invert these cakes while they are still warm.

Walnut, Date, and Pepper Cake

These ingredients may seem fairly mundane, but they have quite a history. They have been exciting the palates of civilized man with their unique blend of flavor since before recorded history.

½ cup (1 stick) unsalted butter

1 cup sugar

3 eggs

1 tsp. vanilla extract

1½ cup all-purpose flour

1 tsp. baking powder

1 tsp. ground black pepper

½ tsp. kosher salt

1 cup dates, pitted and chopped

1 cup walnuts, chopped

Serves 8 to 10
Prep Time: 20 minutes
Cook Time: 45 minutes

1. Preheat the oven to 350°F. Coat six mini bundt pans with nonstick cooking spray.

2. Beat butter and sugar together until smooth and creamy. Add eggs one at a time, then add vanilla.

3. Sift together flour, baking powder, pepper, and salt and stir into batter. Fold in dates and walnuts; transfer batter to the baking dish.

4. Bake until risen and firm, about 20 to 25 minutes. Cool completely.

Helpful Hints

For the spiciest, most flavorful pepper, grind it fresh. If you don't have a pepper grinder, you can crush peppercorns in a coffee grinder or smash them with a frying pan. (Don't whack them! Lean on the pan and rub the peppercorns until they crush.)

Chapter 17

Mini Pies and Tarts

In This Chapter

- ◆ Tarts and pies made in miniature pans
- ◆ Mini tarts and pies made turn-over style
- ◆ Mini pies and tarts filled with chocolate, fruits, and custards

There is nothing more irresistible than pie, unless it's an individual pie, made just for me! The key to a good pie is the crust. Pie crust is not hard, and once you master it, the possibilities are endless.

Cutting in Fat

The cut-in technique is discussed briefly in Chapter 1. However, let's look at it a little more closely, as it is the foundation of American pie.

The technique of combining fat and flour is designed to make the dough flakey. By crumbling in the fat, the butter and flour remain separate. When these small pieces of butter hit the heat of the oven, they release steam, pushing out the nearby dough, creating little pockets of air. It is these pockets of air that create flakiness.

If the flour and butter cream together into a paste, the dough is on its way to becoming a cookie dough. The end product will not be flakey, but crisp. This is not in itself a bad thing, but it is not pie dough.

Keep It Cool

To make successful pie dough you must follow one simple rule: Keep the dough cold. From the time you begin making the dough until it hits the oven, everything about it must remain cold. Cold butter, cold flour, cold water, cold room, cold hands.

If the ingredients are not cold or are allowed to warm up, the tiny pieces of fat will begin creaming together with the flour. As fat softens, it becomes soft and sticky with heat. (Think about the way butter feels directly out of the fridge, versus how it feels after it's been allowed to sit out for a while.)

After the dough is made, keeping it cold while you are working with it will make the dough easier to roll out. The warmer it gets, through the temperature of the room and overhandling, the harder it is to roll. It will stick to the counter, the pin, your hands, and will become the source of much frustration. To combat the problem, work quickly. As soon as the dough shows signs of warming, throw it in the fridge.

Keeping the dough cold is important for baking, too. If the dough is cold when it goes into the oven, it is more likely to hold its shape. Warm dough contains warm fat—which, when heated in the oven, begins to melt immediately. But cold dough, with well-chilled fat, will begin to solidify before the fat gets a chance to melt, and its shape, including decorative edge crimping, will be maintained.

Ingredients

Many bakers prefer to make pie crust with lard. Lard can be cut into the flour in smaller, thinner bits while still remaining separate. However, lard is not as common as it used to be, and many people avoid it because it is a pork product. If you're a lard fan, simply replace the butter in the pie dough recipe with an equal amount of lard. Others prefer the flavor of butter in their pie dough. I like the best of both worlds, and use half lard and half butter. I do not recommend using vegetable shortening in pie dough. It works, but leaves a distinctive aftertaste that I find disagreeable.

Working with Fruit

The success of fruit recipes depends entirely on the quality of the fruit itself. While the flavor of fruit remains fairly constant, the amount of sugar contained within its skin does not. A recipe may require more or less sugar as the sweetness of the fruit varies throughout the year. Additionally, different suppliers, farmers, and markets offer drastically different qualities of the same product.

To combat this variation, use your taste buds. Eat the fruit raw and determine if it needs a lot or a little sugar. Taste it again when sugar is added to be sure you've got enough, and don't be afraid to add more or less sugar than the recipe calls for.

If the fruit you desire is out of season, don't be afraid to use frozen fruit. It is generally of very high quality, picked ripe and flash-frozen right in the orchards and fields. Stay away from canned fruit, which is usually packed with excessively sugary syrup.

Basic Pie Dough

As mentioned in the introduction to this chapter, all elements of this recipe should be kept as cold as possible. On really hot days, I will go so far as to freeze my flour. Every little bit helps.

$\frac{1}{2}$ cup ice water

1 TB. lemon juice

3 cups all-purpose flour

1 tsp. kosher salt

2 TB. sugar

1 cup (2 sticks) unsalted butter, diced and chilled

> **Makes about 2 pounds of pie dough**
>
> **Prep Time:** 20 minutes
>
> **Chilling Time:** 1 hour

1. Combine water, lemon juice, and set aside.

2. In a medium bowl, sift together flour, salt, and sugar, mixing well. Add diced butter and cut in to pea-sized pieces.

3. Add half of the water, stirring with a fork to moisten. Add just enough additional water to hold the dough together.

4. Press dough into a disc, wrap in plastic, and refrigerate for 1 hour. The dough should look marbled, with visible patches of butter and flour. Dough can be refrigerated for 2 days or frozen for up to 1 month.

5. To roll out dough, divide into two or three smaller pieces. Work with only one piece of dough at a time, keeping the remaining dough refrigerated.

6. Knead dough briefly to soften, and form into a disc. Place on a floured surface and, with a rolling pin, roll over the center of dough in one direction.

7. Turn the dough 90° and roll in the center again. Turn again, repeating this pattern until the dough is $\frac{1}{4}$-inch thick. Turning the dough in this manner alerts you right away if it starts sticking to the counter. Spread flour under the dough as necessary to prevent sticking. Work quickly to prevent the dough from warming up. Cut as directed.

Cherry Turnovers

These juicy, sweet treats are best enjoyed warm from the oven. Try them with a scoop of vanilla ice cream, or a dollop of sweetened whipped cream.

4 cups cherries, fresh or frozen, pitted

1 cup sugar, plus more as needed

1 TB. cornstarch

1 tsp. kosher salt

Grated zest and juice of 1 lemon

1 recipe Pie Dough

1 egg

¼ cup sugar

> **Makes 8 to 10 turnovers**
>
> **Prep Time:** 90 minutes
> **Cook Time:** 20 minutes

1. Combine cherries, sugar, cornstarch, salt, and lemon zest and juice. Mix well to thoroughly coat cherries. Taste a cherry to be sure it is sweet enough. If the coating of sugar is not enough, add 2 to 3 tablespoons more as needed. Set aside.

2. Line a baking sheet with parchment paper. Roll dough to ¼-inch thick, and cut a circle that is 4 to 5 inches in diameter. Mix egg with a tablespoon of water, and brush the edges of each circle.

3. Place 1 to 2 tablespoons of cherry filling in the center, fold the dough over into a half circle, and press to seal. Use a fork to create a decorative edge, and place on prepared pan. Repeat with remaining dough, then chill all assembled pies for 30 to 60 minutes, until dough is very cold.

4. Preheat oven to 350°F. Brush top crust with egg wash, and sprinkle with sugar. Bake for 15 to 20 minutes, until golden brown. Tarts can be assembled and frozen raw for up to 2 weeks, then baked directly from the freezer.

Helpful Hints

Cherries ripen in the warm months, usually June through August or September. Look for sweet Bing, Rainier, or Oxheart cherries with glossy bright skin and firm green stems. Canned cherry pie filling is not as good, but fine-quality preserved cherries are often available in better markets. (See Appendix B.)

Brown Sugar Cinnamon Toaster Tarts

I know, I know. These are not really made in the toaster. They are a tribute to the toaster variety.

1 cup (2 sticks) unsalted butter

3²/₃ cups sugar

1 egg

1 TB. milk

2¹/₃ cups all-purpose flour

¾ tsp. baking powder

¼ tsp. kosher salt

1 cup brown sugar

¼ cup cinnamon

2 TB. honey

¼ cup (½ stick) unsalted butter, softened

1 egg

½ recipe White Glaze (Chapter 3)

> **Makes about 6 to 8 mini tarts**
>
> **Prep Time:** 2 hours
> **Cook Time:** 20 minutes

1. Beat together butter and sugar until smooth and creamy. Add egg and milk, mixing thoroughly.

2. Sift together flour, baking soda, and salt and add to mix. Chill dough for 30 to 60 minutes.

3. Combine brown sugar and cinnamon. Set aside 2 tablespoons, then combine remaining with honey and butter, and beat until smooth. Set aside.

4. Line a baking sheet with parchment paper. Roll dough to ¹/₄-inch thick, and cut an even number of 3×4 inch rectangles. Mix egg with a tablespoon of water, and brush the edges of half the rectangles. Place 1 to 2 tablespoons of cinnamon filling in the center.

5. Pierce remaining rectangles decoratively with a fork, lay them on top of the filling, and press to seal. Use a fork to create a decorative edge, and place on prepared pan. Repeat with remaining dough, then chill all assembled tarts for 30 to 60 minutes, until dough is very cold.

6. Preheat oven to 350°F. Brush top crust with egg wash, and bake for 15 to 20 minutes, until golden brown. Brush warm tarts with white glaze, and sprinkle with remaining cinnamon sugar. Tarts can be assembled and frozen raw for up to 2 weeks, then baked directly from the freezer.

Blueberry Pie

Blueberry season peaks in the late summer, but good-quality berries are available frozen year-round. You also can use blackberries or raspberries in this recipe.

4 cups blueberries, fresh or frozen

1½ cups sugar, divided

1 TB. cornstarch

1 tsp. kosher salt

Grated zest and juice of 1 lemon

1 recipe Pie Dough

1 egg

Makes 6 to 8 mini pies

Prep Time: 90 minutes

Cook Time: 20 minutes

1. Combine berries, sugar, cornstarch, kosher salt, and lemon zest and juice. Mix well to thoroughly coat berries. Taste a berry to be sure it is sweet enough. If the coating of sugar is not enough, add 2 to 3 tablespoons more as needed. Set aside.

2. Coat mini pie pans with cooking spray.

3. Roll dough to ¼-inch thick, and cut circles ¼-inch larger than prepared pan. Line pan with circle of dough, and fill to the rim with berries.

4. Mix egg with a tablespoon of water, and brush it onto the edge of the dough. Cut a second circle of dough to fit the top of the pan, lay it on top, and press to seal.

5. Use a fork to create a decorative edge. Repeat with remaining dough, then chill all assembled pies for 30 to 60 minutes, until dough is very cold.

6. Preheat oven to 350°F.

7. Brush top crust with egg wash, and sprinkle with granulated sugar.

8. Bake pie for 20 to 25 minutes, until golden brown and bubbly. Pies can be assembled and frozen raw for up to 2 weeks, then baked directly from the freezer.

Chocolate Cream Pie

Be sure to cool this luscious cream pie before digging in. The creamy chocolate custard is like napalm when it comes right out of the oven.

4 egg yolks

1 cup sugar

⅓ cup cornstarch

4 cups half-and-half

1 TB. vanilla extract

2 oz. bittersweet chocolate

2 TB. unsalted butter

1 recipe Pie Dough

1 egg

¼ cup sugar

½ recipe Chocolate Glaze (Chapter 3)

Makes 8 to 10 turnovers

Prep Time: 90 minutes

Cook Time: 20 minutes

1. In a small bowl, whisk together egg yolks, sugar, and cornstarch, then set aside.

2. In a large saucepan, combine half-and-half and vanilla, then bring to a boil over high heat. At the boil, ladle ½ cup of hot half-and-half into the yolks and whisk quickly to combine.

3. Pour the warmed yolks into saucepan and, over high heat, whisk immediately and vigorously until mixture begins to resemble thick sour cream, about 2 minutes. Remove from heat, adding chocolate and butter, then stir to combine.

4. Strain into a large bowl, cover with plastic wrap pressed directly on the surface, and chill completely.

5. Line a baking sheet with parchment paper. Roll dough to ¼-inch thick, and cut circles 4 to 5 inches in diameter. Mix egg with a tablespoon of water, and brush the edges of each circle.

6. Place 1 to 2 tablespoons of chocolate filling in the center, fold the dough over into a half circle, and press to seal. Use a fork to create a decorative edge, and place on prepared pan. Repeat with remaining dough, then chill all assembled pies for 30 to 60 minutes, until dough is very cold.

Heads Up

For these treats, it's worth taking a little extra time to hunt down some good-quality bittersweet chocolate. Don't use milk chocolate, as it is too pale, and will turn the custard into an unappealing grayish-brown.

7. Preheat oven to 350°F. Brush top crust with egg wash, and sprinkle with sugar. Bake for 15 to 20 minutes, until golden brown. Brush warm tarts with chocolate glaze, then cool completely. Tarts can be assembled and frozen raw for up to 2 weeks, then baked directly from the freezer.

Glazed Apple Turnovers

Nothing beats a homemade apple pie, unless it's these cute handheld pies. They're big enough to satisfy, but small enough so you don't have to share.

5 Fuji apples, peeled, quartered, cored, and sliced

$\frac{1}{2}$ cup brown sugar

1 tsp. kosher salt

1 TB. cinnamon

1 TB. nutmeg

2 to 4 TB. unsalted butter

1 recipe Pie Dough

1 egg

$\frac{1}{2}$ recipe White Glaze (Chapter 3)

Makes 8 to 10 turnovers

Prep Time: 90 minutes

Cook Time: 20 minutes

1. In a large bowl, toss together apples, sugar, salt, and spices. Mix well to thoroughly coat apples.

2. In a large sauté pan over high heat, melt 2 tablespoons butter. Add one layer of apples and cook, stirring often, until tender and caramelized.

3. Transfer apples to a baking sheet to cool, and repeat with remaining apples. Do not crowd apples in pan, or they will cook too slowly and won't caramelize. Cool apples completely.

4. Line a baking sheet with parchment paper. Roll dough to $\frac{1}{4}$-inch thick, and cut circles 4 to 5 inches in diameter. Mix egg with a tablespoon of water, and brush the edges of each circle. Place 1 to 2 tablespoons of apple filling in the center, fold the dough over into a half circle, and press to seal. Use a fork to create a decorative edge, and place on prepared pan. Repeat with remaining dough, then chill all assembled pies for 30 to 60 minutes, until dough is very cold.

5. Preheat oven to 350°F. Brush top crust with egg wash, and sprinkle with sugar. Bake for 15 to 20 minutes, until golden brown. Brush warm tarts with white glaze, then cool before serving. Tarts can be assembled and frozen raw for up to 2 weeks, then baked directly from the freezer.

Tidbits

By pre-cooking the apples, not only do they take on a caramelized flavor, but all excess moisture is eliminated. If raw apples are used, the water in the apple leaks out and makes the turnovers soggy.

Lemon Custard Turnovers

This is perhaps the most popular flavor of all the mini pies. Sweet and tart, it's the sweetheart of snacks.

1 recipe Lemon Curd (Chapter 3)

1 recipe Pie Dough

½ recipe White Glaze (Chapter 3)

> **Makes 8 to 10 turnovers**
>
> **Prep Time:** 90 minutes
>
> **Cook Time:** 20 minutes

1. Line a baking sheet with parchment paper. Roll dough to ¼-inch thick, and cut circles 4 to 5 inches in diameter. Mix egg with a tablespoon of water, and brush edges of each circle.

2. Place 1 to 2 tablespoons of lemon filling in the center, fold dough over into a half circle, and press to seal. Use a fork to create a decorative edge, and place on prepared pan. Repeat with remaining dough, then chill all assembled pies for 30 to 60 minutes, until dough is very cold.

3. Preheat oven to 350°F. Brush top crust with egg wash, and sprinkle with sugar. Bake for 15 to 20 minutes, until golden brown. Brush warm tarts with white glaze, then cool before serving. Tarts can be assembled and frozen raw for up to 2 weeks, then baked directly from the freezer.

Heads Up

The dough should remain cold, but when the time comes to fold the turnovers over, if the dough is too cold, it may crack. This dough warms quickly, so if it seems too cold to bend without breaking, just give it 2 to 3 minutes.

Strawberry Toaster Tarts

These tarts can really brighten your day. Add some sparkle to them by shaking on colored crystal sugar instead of plain granulated sugar before baking.

1 cup (2 sticks) unsalted butter

3²/₃ cups sugar

1 egg

1 TB. milk

2¹/₃ cups all-purpose flour

³/₄ tsp. baking powder

¹/₄ tsp. kosher salt

1 to 2 cups strawberry jam

1 egg

¹/₂ cup sugar

Makes 6 to 8 mini tarts
Prep Time: 90 minutes
Cook Time: 20 minutes

1. Beat together butter and sugar until smooth and creamy. Add egg, milk, and mix thoroughly. Sift together flour, baking soda, salt, and add. Chill dough for 30 to 60 minutes.

2. Line a baking sheet with parchment paper. Roll dough to ¹/₄-inch thick, and cut an even number of 3×4 inch rectangles. Mix egg with a tablespoon of water, and brush edges of half the rectangles. Place 1 to 2 tablespoons of jam in the center.

3. Pierce remaining rectangles decoratively with a fork, lay on top of the filling, and press to seal. Use a fork to create a decorative edge, and place on prepared pan. Repeat with remaining dough, then chill all assembled pies for 30 to 60 minutes, until dough is very cold.

4. Preheat oven to 350°F. Brush top crust with egg wash, and sprinkle with sugar. Bake for 15 to 20 minutes, until golden brown. Tarts can be assembled and frozen raw for up to 2 weeks, then baked directly from the freezer.

Appendix A

Glossary

add-ins A term referring to garnishes folded into dough and batter, such as chocolate chips, nuts, or raisins.

adding alternately A mixing technique in which dry and wet ingredients are divided into three to four portions and added to a batter a little at a time, alternating first the dry mixture and then the wet mixture. The purpose of this technique is even and thorough incorporation (see the explanation in Chapter 1).

almond meal Almonds ground very fine, often used in place of flour.

amaretto An Italian liqueur with the distinctive flavor of bitter almonds.

angel food cake pan A round cake pan with a hollow interior tube that enables heat to penetrate the batter from the middle. The resulting cake has a hole in the center like a giant doughnut.

anise An annual flowering herb related to parsley. The seeds have a distinctive licorice flavor, which is used in liqueurs, candies, sauces, and cosmetics.

blanch To boil briefly and then submerge in ice water to halt cooking. The process is used to loosen skin and intensify the color of vegetables and fruits (also referred to as *parboiling*).

blind bake To prebake a pastry crust or shell that will hold a low-bake or no-bake filling.

buckle Similar to a coffee cake with fruit added to the batter and streusel added to the top.

cake flour A soft flour containing less protein and more starch than all-purpose flour. It's perfect for cakes and other delicate baked goods that don't need a strong, elastic dough structure.

candied ginger Ginger root cooked in sugar syrup and coated with sugar. Often used in baked goods.

caramelized To cook food until the sugar (naturally occurring or added) darkens to an amber "caramel" color. Caramelization brings out the food's deep, sweet, rich flavors.

cassis A black currant berry used to make syrup and liqueur.

citron A large citrus fruit used mainly for its thick peel, which is utilized for its oil and candied for use in baked goods.

clotted cream Thick cream from unpasteurized milk (also known as *Devonshire cream*).

cognac A fine, double-distilled brandy from the town of Cognac and its surrounding regions on the southwest coast of France.

Cointreau An orange-flavored brandy made in France.

confectioner's sugar Another name for powdered sugar (see also *icing sugar*).

creaming A term used to describe the blending of two ingredients into a creamy, smooth, paste-like texture.

crumble A dessert also known as a *crisp*, consisting of fruit with a streusel topping.

currants Tiny raisins made from the miniature *zante* grape. Do not confuse them with red, white, or black currants, which are small berries used for preserves, pastries, and the liqueur *cassis*.

cut-in A method of incorporating fat into dry ingredients by breaking it into small pieces. With heat, moisture is released from the fat, creating a flaky texture. This technique is often used in recipes such as biscuits and pie dough.

Devonshire cream   Thick cream from unpasteurized milk (also known as *clotted cream*).

double boiler   Two pots fitted one on top of the other, designed to allow steam from the bottom to rise and warm the ingredients in the top. Double boilers are used when direct heat is too severe.

egg wash   A glaze made from egg, sometimes with added water, milk, or cream, used to promote the browning of pastries and bread crust.

filberts   Another name for hazelnuts.

foam   A culinary term for anything with air whipped into it; usually eggs, egg yolks, or egg whites.

folding   A technique of incorporating ingredients, usually including a foam, using as few strokes as possible in order to maintain the volume of the mixture.

Fuji   A crisp, sweet Japanese apple variety introduced in the 1960s and popularized in the United States in the 1980s.

ganache   A pastry kitchen staple ingredient made from equal parts cream and chocolate; used for fillings, truffles, glazes, and icings.

gluten   The protein in wheat endosperm that promotes elasticity in bread dough. When moistened and agitated, gluten proteins tighten, creating a smooth, firm dough that can stretch to hold the gas of fermentation.

hard-crack stage   Sugar cooked to between 300°F and 310°F and used in candy and pastry making. When cooled, the sugar will harden and snap or crack easily.

ice bath   Ice water used to quickly cool foods. Foods can be placed in the ice bath directly or set on top in another bowl and stirred until cool.

icing sugar   See *confectioner's sugar.*

macerate   To soak food, usually fruit, in liquid to infuse flavor.

marzipan   A modeling paste made of almond paste, egg white, and powdered sugar, used to create edible figures.

mascarpone   An Italian triple cream cheese, soft like clotted or sour cream and mild in flavor.

microplane A fine grater used for citrus zest and hard cheeses. The tool was originally a carpenter's rasp used for sanding wood.

monounsaturated fat A fat that remains liquid when refrigerated. These fats, in addition to polyunsaturated fats, are found mainly in grain, fish, and soy products. They are considered good fats and should make up 25 percent of your daily fat intake.

Nutella A spread made in Italy from ground hazelnuts and milk chocolate. The product was first developed during World War II as a way to extend rationed chocolate.

omega-3 fatty acids Polyunsaturated fatty acids that are considered essential, meaning that the body must obtain them from your diet because it cannot manufacture them itself. The best sources are fish and flax.

parboiling See *blanch*.

parchment paper Coated paper that withstands heat, water, and grease; used to line pans and wrap foods.

pâte à choux A pastry dough used for making cream puffs, profiter- oles, éclairs, and gougères.

polyunsaturated fats A fat that remains liquid when refrigerated. These fats are found mainly in grain, fish, and soy products. They are considered healthy fats, and in combination with monounsaturated fat intake should comprise 20 percent of your total daily calories.

rancid Oxidation of oil that results in a foul flavor and odor.

reduce A culinary term meaning to cook the water out of a dish, reducing its volume, intensifying its flavor, and thickening its consis- tency.

saturated fats Fatty acids saturated with hydrogen. These fats are solid at room temperature and are mainly found in animal sources, although oil from coconut, cotton, and palm contain high percentages of saturated fatty acids. Intake should be limited to no more than 7 per- cent of total daily calories because saturated fat has been shown to be a major cause of coronary artery disease.

sauté   To cook food quickly over high heat, constantly stirring for even browning. The term comes from the French word meaning "jump," and sauté pans are designed with a curved lip—making constant motion as easy as a flick of the wrist.

seize   A term that refers to the thickening and hardening of melted chocolate that occurs when a small amount of moisture is added.

simple syrup   A pastry staple ingredient made by boiling equal parts sugar and water. It is used for moistening cakes, sweetening sauces and fruit purées, and as a recipe ingredient.

soft-ball stage   Sugar cooked to between 234°F and 240°F and used in candy and pastry making. When cooled, the sugar can be formed into a soft ball.

soft-crack stage   Sugar cooked to between 270°F and 290°F and used in candy and pastry making. When cooled, the sugar is hard but still bends.

stone fruit   A tree fruit that contains a pit, or stone, such as peaches, apricots, cherries, and plums.

Triple Sec   A clear, orange-flavored liqueur.

unsaturated fats   Fat that remains liquid when refrigerated. These fats include polyunsaturated and monounsaturated and are found in olives, canola, avocados, soy, and nuts, as well as fish.

water bath   A method in which a pan of food is cooked while resting in another larger pan of water. The method slows the conduction of heat, cooking the food slowly and gently. The method is known in French as a *bain Marie, and is used when melting chocolate or cooking delicate custards.*

zest   The colorful outermost rind of a citrus fruit containing a high concentration of the essential oils and flavor compounds that flavor the fruit itself.

zester   A small tool designed to strip the aromatic, colorful, oil-rich skin from citrus fruits.

Appendix B

Internet Sources

The following is a compilation of my favorite sources for baking-related merchandise. Happy shopping!

Bakeware

kitchenemporium.com   Mini pans galore, including bundt, muffin, pie, tart, and popover pans—all available in several materials. In addition, this site offers appliances, cookbooks, coffee, tea, and wine products.

kitchenuniverse.com   Paper pans, silicone pans, and fantastically shaped specialty pans.

kingarthurflour.com   A huge selection of bakeware, including mini pans of all kinds, seasonal pans, and bake-and-give paper pans.

pans.com   Cookware, utensils, small appliances, and bakeware made from several materials, including silicone, aluminum, non-stick, cast iron, and glass.

preparedpantry.com   Mini muffin and pie tins as well as ice cream scoops, spades, and nifty ice cream sandwich molds.

Ingredients

barryfarm.com   Candied lemon and citron as well as more unusual candied tropical fruits.

bulkfood.net   A fantastic assortment of extracts, including strawberry, black walnut, and maple.

gourmetshopper.com.au   Lots of spices and flavors, including the hard-to-find candied angelica.

kingarthurflour.com   Not just bakeware, King Arthur carries a wide selection of baking ingredients, including flours, chocolates, and candied lemon and orange peel.

localharvest.org   A variety of organic products, including fresh and preserved fruits, jams, syrups, dried fruits, and juices.

northernbrewer.com   A variety of soda pop extracts, including root beer, cola, cherry cola, and ginger ale.

thespicehouse.com   A great variety of spices plus extracts including coffee, almond, chocolate, and vanilla.

vinetreeorchards.com   Candied citron, lemon peel, and orange peel as well as other dried fruits that are perfect for fruitcakes.

Index